DON'T GO EUROPE!

CHRIS HARRIS

CB
CONTEMPORARY
BOOKS
CHICAGO

Harris, Chris, 1970–
    Don't go, Europe! / Chris Harris.
        p.   cm.
    ISBN 0-8092-3527-7 (pbk.)
    1. Europe—Guidebooks—Humor.   I. Title.
D909.H377   1994
914.04/839—dc20
                                    94-33485
                                       CIP

Author photos by Carolyn Schwarz and Danny Murphy

Based on a real continent.

Published by Contemporary Books, Inc.
Two Prudential Plaza, Chicago, Illinois 60601-6790
Manufactured in the United States of America
International Standard Book Number: 0-8092-3659-1
10   9   8   7   6   5   4   3   2   1

Contents

Author's Note

Bon Jovi! And welcome to the world's first **anti-travel guide**, a book written expressly for you, ***Uglius Americanus***, the honest soul who knows that the real reason "there's no place like home" is because everywhere else *sucks*. We'll tell you where *not* to go, why *not* to go there, and suggest other, better things to do instead.[1] So bid a hearty "Chow" to those *other* guidebooks with snotty, elitist titles like

Europe on the Average, Stinking Proletariat's Yearly Wages a Day

that provide philharmonic orchestra schedules with their listings and rate every nation's food based on how good their **French restaurants** are.

Ditto for those youth-oriented, so-called budget European guides that claim to provide an "alternative experience"; recommend secluded, pristine, untainted-by-any-butt-scratching-Yankee destinations (all of which are, upon the book's publication, immediately overrun by a hundred thousand self-proclaimed alternative experience seekers, mostly of the butt-scratching Yankee variety); and list the meatless routes across the continent as well as all the major hiking trails, as if sampling Europe's different ethnic strains of **poison ivy** is anyone's idea of a fun vacation.

Somewhere in the middle of these two categories lurks the big, grotesque Roger Ebert of travel books, a series of "budget" guides written by Harvard students[2] called ***Let's Go***. These books are known as "The Bibles of the Budget Traveler," not so much because you'll find miniature Gideon *Let's Go*s in the rooms of budget

---

[1]"Hey, what's on TV tonight?"
[2]No, we can't figure it out either.

4

hotels, but more because those who completely ignore their commandments seem to have a lot more fun.

Although other *Let's Go* books are published, including *Let's Go: USA*,[3] *Let's Go: Grab a Beer*, and *Let's Go: MidEast*,[4] the big one is **Let's Go: Europe**, which is so highly regarded that *everyone* seems to take it with them, even if they're *not even going to Europe*, but just to the corner market for a carton of milk.

This 900-page monster describes in detail every single country, city, hotel, restaurant, bar, citizen, pigeon, dirty bath towel, and infectious bacterium in Europe. And just like all other travel guides—up to now—*Let's Go* finds something good to say about everything. **Even France.**

LET'SGOSPEAK:
A QUIK 'N' EZ TRAVEL GUIDE TRANSLATOR

IF A CITY IS DESCRIBED AS	IT'S ACTUALLY
quaint	dull
charming	dull
modern	dirty
traditional	dull, plus no running water
a bustling center of nightlife	dangerous
a healthy mix of new and old	got Vanillaroma fresheners in the outhouses
nestled snugly among the rolling hills of the countryside/snowcapped Alps	200 miles from the nearest Taco Bell
a cross section of many diverse cultures	dull, dull, dull, dull, dull
rich in past glories	rich in present dullness

---

[3]"But wait. . . . We're already *there!*"
[4]"The Koran of the Budget Traveler"

Drop by any city's token **main square statue encircled by steps that tourists sit on** and you'll find gazillions of Ugly Americans sprawled out with their *Let's Go*s, reading about all the sights in that particular city, which is admittedly much easier than tramping around and actually *seeing* all those sights in person.

People follow the gospel of *Go* with a Wacoesque devotion. For example: Two *identical* restaurants can sit next to each other on a street—same crusty dishes, same inflated prices, same overweight maitre d' trying to convince passing tourists that "ze cockaroaches . . . zey are merely pairt of de atmosphere!" But one will be hosting the entire Eastern Seaboard while waiters at the other are playing shuffleboard with dinner plates across the empty tables, all because the first had the luck of being mentioned in *Let's Go*. Science cannot explain why Americans will wait over an hour to be seated at what has obviously become a tourist trap when they could simply go next door and contract salmonella from an undercooked meal with hardly any wait at all.

Don't Go: Europe! is here to change all that.

HOW TO USE THIS BOOK

Seems to us you're already doing a pretty good job!

Whether you're stuck on the wrong side of the Atlantic or safe within the operating radius of your TV remote, *Don't Go* will give you all the dirt you need on Europe, divided, region by region, and in easy-to-find sections. Most of these sections are self-explanatory. However, a few sections may be worth defining more clearly:

Side Note
Provides an interesting side note.

Important Safety Tip
Provides an important safety tip.

Avoid at All Costs
Warns of something to avoid at all costs.

Europe Close-Up

Traveling through Europe, you will find that after a while, many things tend to run into each other.[5] This is because numerous aspects of Europe cross over national borders.[6] Strange, un-American artifacts such as cafés, poodles, soccer, culture, and sophistication may be encountered in many European countries. So throughout the book we present to you these exhaustedly researched essays about such minor faults.

Understanding Those Peculiar Natives

These sections describe the national character, if there is one, and provide helpful hints on how to best communicate with these strange inhabitants, since many of them will have *no conception whatsoever* of American football.

Real Testimony

Often following either of the two sections described above are firsthand accounts of all the awful things that happened to us traveling around Europe, a few of which are even true. We'll introduce you to all sorts of *real Europeans* that will make you want to lock your hotel room door and live off fossilized room-service croissants rather than go outside and risk running into these people. Want to sound well-traveled without straying too far from the fridge? Modify these stories! Pretend they're your own!

Lamb, Lamb, Lamb

In short, if a troop of Iranian terrorists were to abduct you and forcibly ship you to Europe with the intention of driving you to the Mideast in order to use you as some three of diamonds in the great poker game of international terrorism, but European road signs confused them so much that they ended up in this city instead, and they just decided to set you free here because your ceaseless and rather unfair complaint "lamb, lamb, lamb, nothing but lamb" offended the poor cook, who was only doing his best under the circumstances after all, then *as long as you're here, you may as well consider this activity, but in no way should this otherwise change your mind about not going.*

---

[5]like Italian drivers
[6]like Romanians

Disclaimer

Any facet of our book that bears resemblance to actual people or countries in Europe is entirely coincidental.

Finally, we want you to know that, as they say in England, "As they say in America, 'It's all for fun and games.'" Europe isn't really all that bad, and the United States isn't really a whole lot better than any European country.[7]

And now, our feature presentation . . .

---

[7]Except France. We actually are better than them.

Introduction

Brussels, Berlin, Copenhagen!
London, Paris, Florence, Rome!
Nice, Madrid, Vienna, Prague an'—
What? No "Melrose"? Let's Go: Home!

Don't Go! Stay at home! Those snooty Harvard students who write *Let's Go: Europe* wouldn't know Köln from Cologne. Europe's a dump! Take your worst nightmare, add the **French**, and boom—you've got Europe.

Besides, you live in *America*, buddy—Number One Greatest Country in the World, home of cheesesteaks, David Hasselhoff, popcorn chicken, the Thighmaster, deficit spending, and syndicated "Who's The Boss?" Okay, "Herman's Head" was canceled, we lost at our national pastime to the Canadians (Eh?) of all people, and our country's harmony has been strained by recession, shattered by racial violence, and bastardized by Wilson-Phillips—granted. But this is the *U.S.A.*, and even if it does have its minor faults,[1] you can be proud that no other country comes even *close* to matching our selection of cable stations.

Don't Go! Stay at home! Why waste all that precious moulah on a fleeting two-week trip when you could spend it on something more enduring, like **100 Nintendo cartridges**? Sure, it may have been important once, but now Europe is just a washed-up tumor on the continent of Asia—yes, washed-up! How do we know? Just ask one of them, "You're a peon?"

And they'll say, "Why yes, I am!"

Besides, Europe offers nothing, we repeat *nothing*, that can't be found within the comfort of our own local fast-food establishments. Observe the table on the following page:

---

[1]e.g., most of Ohio

IF YOU'RE INTERESTED IN AN ATTRACTION OF EUROPE LIKE	THEN CHECK OUT
Irish culture	McDonald's
Monarchical societies	Burger King
Outdated architecture	Howard Johnson's
Vast stretches of unpopulated regions	Also Howard Johnson's
Italian food	Pizza Hut
Long, mysterious history	Wendy's Old-fashioned Hamburgers
Thriving underground economy	Subway Subs
Castles	(Hint: square hamburgers)
Interesting artifacts from backward lands	Kentucky Fried Chicken

Ooooooh, but it's the *people* you're interested in, is it? Well *sure*, traveling around Europe is a great way to meet many diverse **other Americans traveling around Europe**. But don't expect to speak with anyone from anyplace weirder than Wisconsin.[2]

Why not? *Europeans don't like you.* They know you. Thousands of pot-bellied, Polaroid-snapping, extra-ketchup-asking-for, polyester-Hawaiian-shirted ambassadors from our nation have preceded you. And they have *not* given you a good rep. You, my friend, are the **Ugly American**. Aren't you?

Foreign tourists, you can bet, don't do any of these things when they visit *our* country. We seem to shoot them before they get a chance.

Don't Go! Stay home! America is full of unexplored culture—or are you forgetting **South of the Border** theme park? C'mon, have you ever been to the **Gilroy Garlic Festival**? Made your obligatory pilgrimage to the **sacred burial grounds of Elvis A. Presley**? Gotten mugged in **New York**? No? Then why go to Europe? Haven't you *heard* about this place?

---

[2] a state here in the U.S.

DON'T GO'S COSMO-STYLE PERSONAL SURVEY QUIZ: ARE YOU AN UGLY AMERICAN?

1. When attempting communication with indigenous Europeans, one should address them

a) in their own language.

b) with a long series of exaggerated arm gestures and apelike pointing.

c) real loud, 'cause sometimes their English, it ain't so good.

2. What statement best describes your fashion philosophy?

a) I try to dress appropriate to whatever culture I'm visiting.

b) Sometimes I feel like I have nothing to wear because all of my "Burn This!" American flag T-shirts are dirty.

c) Dark socks go really well with my Bermudas.

3. You have been given a foreign-language dictionary as a going away gift. You

a) devote yourself to learning the subtle nuances of the language.

b) look up all the swear words, then chuck it.

c) give it to people you meet on your trip who don't know English, so they can look up your questions and then answer you in your own language.

4. What souvenir(s) are you most likely to bring back from Europe?

a) chocolates, museum picture books, and other cultural artifacts

b) beer steins, road signs, hotel soap, and pieces of any major monument

c) a plastic "yodeling Yingä" pen whose lederhosen come off when you turn it upside down

After filling out all the questions, add up your total score: a = 1, b = 2, c = 3. If you actually do this, then you are an Ugly American.

• Y'know what they still call dance clubs over there? ***Discos***. Yeah, *discos*. Sure, you may think it's only a name—just wait 'til you get your earring caught in some guy's California-shaped sideburn.

• Typical waiter: "Ice? You wantah yoor bayverahzj vith ice? Hahahahahahahahaha. Ahem. No! Spit! Spit!"

• **No peanut butter.** Instead, they have this **chocolate-nut paste** called Nutella. Ever tried a Nutella-and-jelly sandwich? It's like a Brach's candy display between two pieces of bread. And while you're at it, you can say goodbye to Taco Bell, corn dogs, Heinz 57, Cool Ranch Doritos, Pringles, Mr. Pibb, pretzel sticks, potato sticks, Pixie Stix, Dum-dums, Cheez Whiz, Cheez Doodles, Cheez Puffs, Cocoa Puffs, Fudgsicles, Doo-dads, Twinkies, Jolt cola, and, yes, Marshmallow Fluff. The French don't even know what Fluff *is*.

They epitomize it, sure. They just don't know what it is.

And the only Cheerios you'll get are from Brits waving you goodbye. One wonders how Europeans keep from starving.

• All the men, even the old, overweight, Bavarian-beer-bellied fathers, wear these *leee*tle bikini-brief bathing suits. Our advice: Keep your eyes shut until the "boxer rebellion" makes its way over here.

• Europe's motto: "If you're old enough to breathe, you're old enough to smoke!" Fortunately, the smell is somewhat hidden because Europeans generally do not believe in deodorant.

We're telling you, folks, Don't Go! If you have to visit another continent, pick someplace more hospitable, like **Antarctica**. But not Europe. Never Europe.

THE MANY, MANY FLAGS OF EUROPE

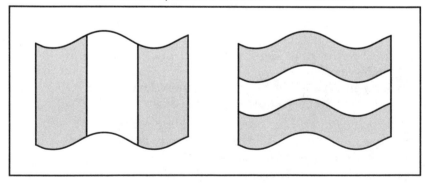

Not Planning Your Trip

Don't Go strongly advises against any intentional travel to Europe. However, as they say, "accidents and momentary bouts of stupidity will happen," and just as with other unforeseen disasters—**fires, earthquakes, plagues of locusts, rivers turning to blood, Republican domestic policy**—one should know what to do in case of emergency. To this end, we provide the following tips on Europe preparedness.

PACKING

Packing would be simple and painless, and people would do it just for fun on occasion were it not for the dreaded **justincase effect**:

> **"Well, I hate this dress and I haven't worn it in three years, but what if *ochre* is the hip color in Akron? Better bring it along, *justincase*. Aaand *justincase* I get invited scuba diving, I'll go ahead and pack this *oxygen tank* too. . . ."**

While packing, keep in mind that as you travel through Europe, little gremlins will be sneaking up to your luggage and hiding small pieces of lead in hard-to-find places, gradually making it so heavy that you will be forced to stop and search all the compartments, wondering if Dan Aykroyd somehow slipped in your backpack while you weren't looking.

Here's a simple rule of thumb for packing on a long trip: Just pack everything you think you'll need; then take out half; walk around the block with what's left to test its weight; add some bricks to represent souvenirs, street signs, chunks of the Berlin Wall, and small pieces of lead you'll be picking up while there; walk with it again; remove one more item per each day of travel; add more money; divide the angle bisector by the hypotenuse squared; and let chill for one hour. If your pack is still too heavy, then take everything out, and consider checking the movie listings instead.

Here are a few other necessary items:

• **A valid U.S. passport**[1] with your full name and recent photo that depicts what you would look like if under the influence of illegal substances. According to U.S. Customs regulations, looking too much like your passport photo is sufficient grounds to bring out the **sniffy dogs** and search your belongings.

• **A padlock** with which to lock your luggage to something sturdy while you're sightseeing, so that when someone steals it they'll ruin the straps or a zipper clamp.

• **A neck pouch** in which to hold your valuables. This is virtually foolproof against the simple native muggers who will naively think, "I won't mug *that* American, 'cause the ones with large growths on their chests *never* seem to be carrying any valuables with them when I ask."

• *Let's Go: Europe*—this in itself will require an extra backpack, although some travelers conserve energy with the "Let Go: Europe" method: After you've visited any city or country, rip out the pages that discuss it from *Let's Go* and throw them away. When all you have left is the cover and shady Single Engine Charter Cargo Planes "R" Us travel agency ads, then you know you've been away too long.

MONEY

is recommended.

Many people bring **American Express Travelers' Cheques** with them because the TV tells them to. This is usually a good reason. However, we have noticed something pretty suspicious: *Every time* someone on TV is traveling with American Express Travelers' Cheques, *they get robbed.*

You'll be much better off if you simply stuff **wads of $20 bills** in your socks and underwear. There's nothing quite like peeling a sweaty greenback off a pile of reeking, putrid cash that's been collecting foot bacteria for the past two weeks and giving it to some German banker to exchange. Have fun!

---

[1]or reasonable facsimile

LANGUAGES

One of the first things you'll notice about Europeans is that they talk funny. This is because they speak entirely different **languages**, much like those characters on PBS specials or "Beverly Hills 90210." Over a hundred different languages are spoken in Europe, and *Let's Go* suggests learning *all* of them before visiting Europe.

Yes, it is a sad statement that in this modern day and age, English is still considered a second language in some parts of the world. But some people choose to help the natives by learning *their* language before going. This is a very admirable, Peace Corps–type option, although it does mean taking a class and reading books, so you may want to reconsider.

Europe Close-Up: Language Textbooks

All classroom language books follow the same format. In the first chapter, you meet a few characters with dorky names that will haunt you like a veggie burrito through the rest of the book. This is certain to be unsettling, for at the beginning of the book it is painfully clear that these people have all the character depth of a corn flake. Take this *actual complete first-chapter dialogue* translation from a French lesson book:

Michel:	*Bonjour, Guy.*	Hello, Guy.
Guy:	*Bonjour, Michel. Ça va?*	Hello, Michel. How are you?
Michel:	*Oui ça va, et toi?*	Fine, thank you. And you?
Guy:	*Pas mal.*	Not bad.

That's their entire conversation—he sure is one wild and crazy Guy!

We think a much more realistic first dialogue would go something like this:

Michel:	*Bonjour, Guy. Pourquoi as-tu un si bête nom?*	Hello, Guy. Why do you have such a stupid name?
Guy:	*Bonjour, Michel. Au moins mon nom ne sonne pas comme une jeune fille.*	Hello, Michel. At least my name doesn't sound like a girl's.
Michel:	*Ah oui? Bien comment sonne un sandwich de knûckle?*	Oh yeah? Well, how does a knuckle sandwich sound?
Guy:	*Pas mal.*	Not bad.

Fortunately, the dialogues do not long remain at fetus reading level. As one flips through the book, these characters mysteriously become smarter and smarter so that even though they can't feed themselves until chapter five, by the end of the book, they'll be having deep philosophical debates about NAFTA.

Not that it matters. You may have spent four years of high school Spanish discussing the desk of your Aunt Totie, but you may as well have just taken the extra hours of **shop** as you'll see as soon as you touch down in Madrid. The American version of languages is about as natural as the American version of **cheese**. After all, you know what they say,

Accents will happen.

Don't Go's One Immutable Law of Nature is that there is **no way to be cool** when speaking a foreign language. One of our favorite scenes of all time was when this German came up to a friend of ours in a bar here in America and suavely asked her, "So, do you arrive many times at here?"

Well, we know what you're thinking by now: "Hey, if languages are so tough to learn, and everyone in Europe speaks English anyway, then why should I even bother trying to learn their sissy languages?"

That's it! Now you're catching on!

Now some of you skeptics out there might be thinking, "Well, yeah, but what about **Esperanto**? Isn't that worth learning?" Well, let us tell you a bit about Esperanto.

DONT GO'S FUN QUIZ

Esperanto is
a) that annoying song by the Eagles ("Esperantooooo, why don't you come to your senses?").
b) a café drink ("I'd like a double decaf esperanto, please").
c) "the international language."

If you picked letter c, then you're a **nerd**, because you're **right**! Esperanto is an artificially induced language created to unite the world. So far it's united Poland, Russia, and Portugal, and maybe thirty people anywhere else. Its users should be getting a little *desperanto* about its future by now, if you ask us.

THE GENERIC EUROPEAN CITY

European cities all start to look the same after a while. This is because they *are* all the same. Consider the following recipe as a preview of *wherever* you plan to visit.

DON'T GO'S
HOMEMADE EUROPEAN CITY DELIGHT

INGREDIENTS

1 big ol' famous church near the center that took centuries to construct

3–4 truckloads other, not-quite-as-famous-but-still-not-to-be-missed churches and synagogues to taste

1 famous bridge that supposedly used to be romantic crossing a river that supposedly used to be unpolluted

6 blocks ritzy, overpriced main drag filled with wealthy out-of-towners taking pictures of each other and thinking they're all locals

2 square miles quaint, older, cobblestone pedestrian roads, known as the Old City

1 large town square, sufficient in size to hold the old town hall and 4–7 mimes without crowding

1 tall monument or hill with a breathtaking view, closed for repairs

1 grand palace/castle, either in or right near the city, from which some slightly mad king once ruled over half of Europe

500,000 arrogant local residents who would rather you not intrude upon their city which, although it is quickly being destroyed by you damn tourists, is still the greatest in the world

DIRECTIONS

1. Combine all ingredients except residents; let stand 4–6 hundred years. Shake up occasionally with outside force.
2. Meanwhile, mold residents until set firmly in ways. Sprinkle throughout city.

VARIATIONS:

Northern Style: Wrap residents in long underwear; put to work immediately.

Southern Style: Lay residents flat; sun-dry until desired thickness is reached.

Eastern Style: Place all residents in center square; shake well.

Serves 6,000–8,000 tourists

Not Getting There

A number of equally effective means of not getting to Europe are available for today's American. Perhaps the most convenient is the **armchair**, although the roomier **bed** also has its proponents.

A wide variety of other, less popular devices—the **Jacuzzi**, **bungee cord**, and **industrial dryer**, for example—also exist. *When used properly*, they are almost certain not to transport one to the Old Country. However, choose carefully. Each method may involve its own time commitment, expenses, or troublesome hassles, such as sudden and painful death.

Every year, a large number of ill-advised homebodies attempt to not visit Europe by **airplane** and ten hours later find themselves standing on the runway of a foreign country against their every will and intention. *We do not recommend traveling by plane as a way of not reaching Europe.* It is expensive, cramped, and *very* risky compared with other means available.

AIRPLANES

As you board the plane, you should be able to locate your seat by following the sounds of the **complimentary howling children**, conveniently placed within strangling range on either side of your seat. (Remember, in case of emergency, place the oxygen mask on *yourself* first, and *then* strangle the howling children.) These kids will make you bury your head in your **complimentary synthetic pillow**, twist on your **complimentary recycled air vent**, and beg the attendant for a **complimentary shot of morphine**. To avoid them, *Don't Go* suggests booking a seat where they're less likely to be, like the **smoking section** or the **cargo bin**.

Entertainment

Airlines long ago discovered that passengers won't at all mind a bumpy, noisy, delayed, turbulent flight if mindless distractions are provided that are so unbearable in and of *themselves* that they will make the flight itself seem like a Swedish massage by comparison. Here are some examples:

The complimentary headphones: These are special prewaxed earpieces through which one can hear the "In the Spotlight: Waylon Jennings" channel, the New Age babbling brook relaxation station, or the **dance music channel** (Dance music?).

The complimentary movie: After a number of flights, our researchers have finally discovered how this works. In the back of each flight's complimentary magazine (see below) are listed the six movies that the airline is showing. Five of these are brand-new, critically acclaimed blockbuster hits that you haven't seen yet but really, really want to—all playing on the flights going in the direction opposite from you. The sixth is **The Three Amigos**, which is what *you* get.

The complimentary meal: We asked some folks to think up some positive things to say about airplane food instead of rehashing the same old jokes, and this is what we came up with: "Mmmmm, good peanuts!"

Airplane food has made some progress in recent years. In the olden days, it was an unrecognizable, disgusting mound of crusty guck. Nowadays, one can very often recognize it ("Ah! This disgusting mound of crusty guck must be my complimentary meal!").

The complimentary magazine: On a six-hour flight, your average bookless passenger will pick up the complimentary magazine, flip through it hopelessly for about 20 seconds, and put it away again approximately 653 times, each time wishing she'd brought along something more worth reading, such as a milk carton. Instead, she ends up skimming through an interview with the CEO of some drugstore chain, an essay with a title like "The World's at Your Fingertips with Laptop Computers" and a pictorial titled "Fresno, Pittsburgh of the West."

Not even the **complimentary half-filled-in crossword** is any help. It was recently discovered that airplane magazines are *published* with the crosswords half finished, written in pen, with mostly wrong answers, just to make you think that the guy who sat in your seat before you had the brain capacity of a Cheerio. That way you won't complain about *The Three Amigos*, thinking, "Well, they obviously have to appeal to some pretty stupid people on these flights."

The complimentary hot towel: Although no one has ever come out and admitted it and formed a support group for those who feel the same way, we here at *Don't Go* believe that this is secretly everyone's favorite part of an airplane flight.[1]

The complimentary nervous older woman sitting next to you who's never ridden on an airplane before: "I'm sorry, we're all out of the complimentary overweight businessman in the sweaty, wide-collared yellow shirt. Will the nervous older woman be all right?"

Everything on an international flight is complimentary, except for the passengers' comments when they finally get off it.

---

[1] unless one has never seen *The Three Amigos*

Not Getting Around

Let's face it—the only good way of getting a-round in Europe is at an English pub.

But some people were, as they say in Norway, "bjørn to møve," so if you find yourself in Europe and would rather not hide out in your hotel until it's all over—like we did—then here's the scoop on getting around.

BY PLANE

Please. We have **congressional districts** that are bigger than Europe. Take the train.

BY TRAIN

Trains are the most popular means of travel for tourists in Europe because they provide an opportunity to interact with *real Europeans* as you frantically claw at their eyeballs trying to get the last free seat. Traveling on **overnight trains** is especially fun, because you can bring all your belongings into a compartment, go to sleep, and wake up the next morning in a **completely different environment**, such as a compartment with *none* of your belongings in it.

There are three choices of sleeping quarters for these rides, depending on your budget:

The plain ol' seat: an inexpensive bed in which you will get very little sleep.

The couchette: a moderately expensive bed in which you will get very little sleep.

The private chamber: an extremely expensive bed in which you will get very little sleep. (The *reason* you will get very little sleep is that **train conductors**, who seem to have nothing better to do at

3:00 A.M., come by every hour asking for tickets that you've already shown them. That kills them. . . . We almost did too.)

The **plain ol' seat** is a spot in a train compartment with two sets of three seats facing each other. During overnight rides these seats can be pushed flat so that six people can lie across them, alternating, so that each head is conveniently resting between two pairs of rancid feet that have logged 80 walking miles in the past four days without a change of socks. The socks on said feet are by now, through a combination of sweat, dirt, and festering microbes, permanently attached to said feet.

Unless you're a member of the Sam Walton family, you will not be able to afford **private chambers**. That leaves the *couchette*, a French word meaning "slab of unstable plywood hanging from a train wall."

The *couchette* (six are stacked in each train compartment, with three against each wall) is the Frenchman's revenge against Americans, ingeniously designed to magnify every single jerk and jolt of the train so that you will afterwards wish you had slept *anywhere else*, like on a mechanical bull.[1]

If you travel alone by *couchette*, you'll usually find yourself in a compartment with a family of five. But not just any old family of five—a big, bold, rugged, "back to nature" Swiss Family Robinson Crusoe family of five that's in the middle of its six-month backpacking "tour of everywhere in Europe that doesn't have a Laundromat." This family will get on the train not where you did, but at the one boonyville layover that the train makes around two in the morning. They'll trudge in, tromp mud all over your belongings for a while, and yell things like "Dashenfuchenagenlafen? Ja, ja! Ha! Ha! Ha!" at each other for about an hour while preparing for bed.

 ### Real Testimony: Midnightmare Express
Our undercovers reporter checked out the sleep scene for *couchettes* on a Paris-Berlin trip. Here's his "As soon as I find a real bed I'm gonna sleep like a" travelogue:

9:00 I get on the train, find the right compartment, and grab a middle *couchette*. The train leaves, and I'm the only person so far in my compartment. I dance a little Irish jig, I'm so happy.

---
[1]or an airplane flight

10:00 I retire for night. I turn out the light, climb into plywood (What, no mint on my pillow?), and lie as perfectly still as possible, which is not very.

10:10 WHAM! Door opens, conductor takes my ticket.

11:10 WHAM! Another ticket check. No problem. I doze off. . . .

2:00 WHAAP! Surprise! The entire Von Trapp family slams on the light and tumbles into my compartment, singing and shouting and farting and having a great time all around. I close my eyes and hope the illusion will go away until I hear a CRACK! above me as the 300-pound, lederhosen-laden father hoists himself up onto the *couchette* above mine. I spend the rest of the night in mortal fear that he will come crashing down upon me at any second.

2:20 WHAM! Ticket check.

3:00 I wake up sweating. Hot enough für ja? I remove the blanket, peel off my T-shirt, and try not to inhale too much Eurosweat.

3:30 CRACK! The father climbs down and FWWP! opens the window. CRACK! He climbs back up.

3:45 I wake up, freezing. I put on my soggy T-shirt, pull over the blanket, and curl up in a tight ball.

4:00 SLAM! The mother closes the window.

4:10 WHAM! Ticket check.

4:30 I wake up, sweating. I lose the blanket, remove my T-shirt, and try to think cool thoughts.

4:45 CRACK! SQUISH! "OW!" "Entschuldigung." Herr Von Trapp, climbing down to open the window, steps on my arm. I am not enjoying this night. THUD! He jumps down the rest of the way, almost crashing through the train floor in the process, FWWP! opens the window, and CRACK! climbs back up, managing to avoid most of my limbs this time.

5:00 I wake up freezing, put on my T-shirt, feel for the blanket, and realize that it's fallen to the floor. So I grab a dress shirt from my bag, throw it over myself, and again curl up in a tight ball.

5:15 SLAM! Mom strikes again.

5:30 I wake up sweating. I throw everything off and lay awake, limbs against the wall, waiting for all 300 pounds of Dad to jump down and open the window again.

6:10 WHAM! Ticket check.

6:30 Still waiting for Dad. The heat, smell, and lack of sleep have all combined to make me a little delirious. For a moment I imagine I'm a piece of pepperoni trapped inside an overmicrowaved pocket pizza.

7:00 Still waiting. I finally drift into a restless slumber. . . .

7:18 WHAM! The conductor tells us we've arrived. I bid a hearty one-fingered farewell to my pals and shuffle out to the nearest park bench.

BY CAR

Car rentals are another option, and those who have heard that renting a car is extremely expensive in Europe will be relieved to find out that the cost of the car is *nothing* compared to what they'll be paying for **gas**. Gasoline in Europe is sold by the liter, also known as a **wimp gallon**, but it may be more economical to simply import your own oil field.

A few other warnings:

European road signs: These should cause you absolutely no trouble because they *don't exist.* You can drive for hours trying to get to Belgium and the only clue you'll get that you're going the wrong way is the increasing number of Cyrillic[2] license plates you see.

Driving rules: The British are the only people who do not drive on the right side of the road; they drive on the *wrong* side. This rule does not include Italians, who in general are hitting under par if they find the road at all.

Speed limits: When they exist, they are often high enough to prove Einstein's theories. This is why European scientists have no major atom smashers or supercolliders—they simply wait by the side of

---

[2] a type of paint used for writing the Russian alphabet

the autobahn for an accident. And since most European back roads are not wide enough to qualify as a deer path in the U.S., every time two cars approach each other it's a split-second chicken fight to see who'll keep going and who'll have to pull off the road into the vineyard.[3] It takes a steady hand. . . . One moment of fear and boom—you're the next **Princess Grace.**

 Mountain roads in Europe are literally **five inches wide** and have *no safety railing.* Once, we were sitting at the "last chance curb" at the bottom refusing to go any farther, when we saw one of those rickety Third World–country **local buses** carrying about 300 natives and **real live chickens and goats** inside come barreling around the last turn, with literally **three wheels** hanging in midair over the edge and various pieces of luggage and furniture flying off the top into the valley below. Well, that got us all fired up. "If they can do it, so can we!" we shouted. We started up the car, drove a few more feet, decided that if we were *really* brave then we wouldn't feel any need to test it, and took the scenic route through the valley instead.[4]

A HELPFUL PHRASE FOR MOTORISTS IN EUROPE:

"But officer, I was only going one way!"

"Mais officeur, j'etait seulement allé un chemin! "
"Aber Offizier, ich war nur ein weg gegehen!"
"Butt afuoco, andavo solo uno via!"

BI CYCLE (OR EUROPE ON 20 STITCHES A DAY)

Cycling is a wonderful way to get a close-up view of Europe's landscape. Real close-up. As in, "Boy, the tar on this road doesn't look anything like how it tastes!"

It's not that European drivers are openly malicious to cyclers. They're *just bad drivers.* As the Bible says, "It is easier for a camel

---

[3]or off the Alps
[4]A common road sign in the valley: WATCH OUT FOR FALLING ARMOIRES

to pass through the eye of a needle than it is for an Italian to stay in his lane." So cyclists in Europe are pretty much on a par with the American **squirrel**:

Le Driveur:	La de da, hmm . . .
Le Passengeur:	Oh, watch out, dear. There's a cyclist—.
Le Cycliste:	WAH! [thrmp!]
Le Driveur:	[swerving car a bit, glancing in rearview mirror] Whoops. Do you see it behind us?
Le Passengeur:	No. Oh, I hope you didn't hit the poor thing. . . . Now what's that noise?
Le Cycliste:	[flmp, flmp, flmp, flmp . . .]

Of course this couldn't really happen—bicycles are actually bigger than most European cars. Have fun, and remember:

 Stick to the side of the road, or you'll end up sticking all over it.

BY FOOT

One can also **hitchhike** in Europe if one is especially short of cash or higher brain functions, but because we want to make the **Germany** chapter as big BIG **BIG** as possible, we have chosen to discuss it there.

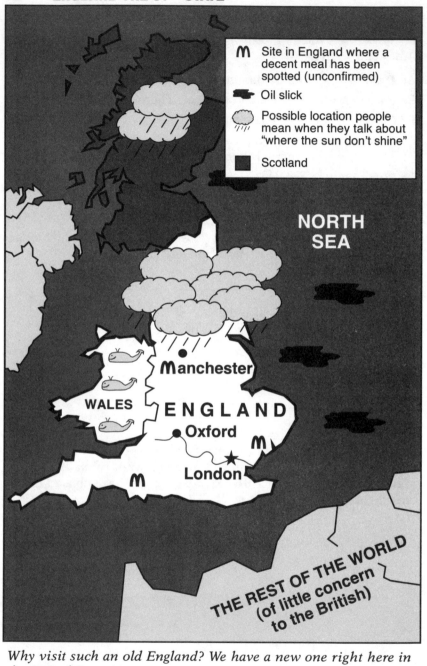

Why visit such an old England? We have a new one right here in the United States!

England
The 51st State

India, Australia, Africa's eastern side—
Their colonies once gave the British smiles.
Now they've lost it all and so they have to
*   hone their pride,*
By colonizing sheep on Falkland Isles.

ENGLAND
VITAL INFORMATION

Exchange rate: 1 pound sterling = 1 quid =
1 sovereign = 20 shillings = 100 pence = 200 ha'pennies =
2 much trouble!

Dominant stereotype: Priggish, long-faced, albino,
tea-sipping queen lovers with no sense of humor except for
that John Cleese guy who's actually pretty funny I guess

Official motto: "Mind your teas and queues"

Theme song: "Ain't No Sunshine"

For fun: What?

Contributions to American culture: Ob-la-di,
Heath Bar Crunch, Ob-la-da, and really boring, "Boy, I
wonder if *this* author got paid by the word" 19th-century
novels about rich aristocrats who run into poor people that
by amazing coincidences turn out to be related to them

Ugly American visits, returns with: Plastic
Big Ben; mini-Stonehenge construction set; peculiar affinity
for the word *poppycock*

Overall rating (−10 to 0): −7

**How to sound like you've really, truly
been there:** "Awrgh! Royght! Harrumph! Quoite quoite,
rather jolly jolly good and awl 'at bloody rubbish. Cheerio!"
(Alternative selection: "Whew! No *wonder* the Pilgrims
risked their lives to get out of there!")

England, also known as Pretty OK Britain, The United Kingdom of
America, and Home of the Bee Gees, is a funny little island filled
with people who are *almost* Americans but not quite, much like
those you'll find in Canada or Texas.

The primary ethnicity in England is neither white, black, red,
nor yellow, but sort of pasty. Englanders are readily identified in
the wild by their overtraditional stuttering and firm conviction that
punk music is still cool. This is not to say that England doesn't have

its advantages over the rest of Europe. It's closer to the U.S., for example.

History

Too much history, not enough nookie. That's the British in a nutshell. English history is nothing but a long series of madcap power trips by large men with roman numerals for last names, the closest to which we've had in our country is the *Rocky* series, or possibly **Malcolm**.

Some of England's most famous rulers were King Pleading V, Queen Bottomov IX, King Larry the Live, King Tom the Unusually Spritely for This Time of Day, and Sally, Queen of Mustangs.

England was also active in the arts and sciences. **Shakespeare**, known for writing **plays whose titles give away the ending** (*Love's Labor's Lost, All's Well That Ends Well, The Butler Did It*), lived here. So did **Newton**, a man whom King George the Curious claimed had "more gray matter in his head than in all the Taco Bell food I've eaten in my life!" According to legend, Newton was resting under a tree one day when an apple fell on his head, thus leading to the discovery of the **concussion**.

The Magna Carta, 1066, and the **Spanish Armada** also happened, although who exactly gives a flip has not yet been determined.

This brings us right up to the Most Important Thing That Ever Happened To England.[1] The British tend to downplay the significance of what we all know was the biggest historical event *ever*, choosing to stress their own generosity and goodwill in (Harrumph!) *granting* us our freedom, rather than dwelling upon the minuscule detail that we in fact whipped their little red-tailed behinds.

For this reason, they often call the Revolution by less glorious, less flattering names, such as the **Freeing of the Yanks** or the **War of the Amicable Separation.** Call it what you will. England lost thanks to two main factors:

1. Their use of **redcoat soldiers**, who thought that wearing bright clothing and marching in rows was pretty clever war strategy.
2. The indefatigab—you know what I'm trying to say—**American spirit**, led by such patriots as **John Hancock**, whose signature alone was enough to subdue an entire division of British soldiers, and

---

[1] the American Revolution

Patrick Henry, whose rallying cry of "Give me liberty or give me a beer!" spurred **Thomas Jefferson** to stay home and write A Very Important Essay, even though it was the Fourth of July and Martha had already made potato salad. This was **the Declaration of Independence**, and its timeless opening lines[2] still move the hearts of millions each year.

Well, once they lost us, you could just hear the fat lady clearing her throat. The insecure Brits went continent hopping, each time trying to "civilize" the natives by offering them a lifetime of tea and servitude in exchange for assuring the English that yes, don't worry, they *are* the peak of civilization—each time getting laughed off the face of the continent by the uncivilized natives. Today it is not so much the United Kingdom as the *Untied* Kingdom.

Without all this history, England would never be where it is today—namely, **stuck in the past**. The British are notoriously *traditional*, which is the polite way of referring to a group of has-beens clinging desperately to ancient customs like fox hunts and afternoon tea and judges with large hairpieces. The *only* changing Brits feel comfy with these days is that of the **guard**.

 Food

Unless you count "squishy," British food cannot easily be summed up in a single word like that of Italy ("pasta"), France ("slugs"), or Poland ("no"). Chefs in England have mastered the fine art of taking such mouthwatering ingredients as **exotic fresh meats** and **crisp, ripe vegetables** and reducing them to an overcooked, tasteless pile of gray **mush**. They pride themselves on achieving the texture and flavor of microwaved food without sacrificing the lengthy cooking times of the conventional boiling pot.

We here at *Don't Go* have obtained a British cookbook with recipes that would make *Silence of the Lambs*'s Hannibal Lecter nauseous. One particular chapter lists dishes that use random "other parts of the animal," collectively known as—get this—**offal**. We say, "You bet it is!" Some of the *real, honest-to-God* highlights:

Oxtail: "It should look fresh when bought, with good red flesh and creamy white fat."
Hearts: "Wash thoroughly and remove all the tubes and arteries."
Sweetbreads: We here at *Don't Go* aren't even sure what these are,

---

[2]"Got a call from an old friend/We used to be real close"

but the book says "allow one pair per portion" and "remove the veins and skin [and] place the blanched sweetbreads between two plates to flatten them." Being the insecure masculine kind of editors that we are, we are frankly quite worried about what sweetbreads are, and we'll sock any Brit who tries to touch *our* sweetbreads. And they'd better stop calling us "mate," too.

Brains: "Calves' brains should be soaked in cold water for 15 minutes. . . . Remove and take off membrane before continuing." Trust us on this one: A mind is a terrible thing to taste. Now we understand why **Gandhi** fasted until the British left his country.

Practical Information

Climate: All other guidebooks call Britain's weather unpredictable. Poppyseed! We here at *Don't Go* found the **torrential downpour** quite stable. "The sun never *rises* on the British Empire," if you ask us. This lack of sun also explains why Brits tend to be, on the average, whiter than David Duke's hiney.

Courtesy: The British are very courteous[3] toward each other and expect the same degree of stuffed-up dryness from their visitors. Here's an old four-step method for learning the **proper way to address all Brit types**:

1. What do you breathe?
2. What's on top of your head?
3. Where does a lion live?
4. Now, say it all together, and you've got it!

If that's all too complex, then a simple "Hey, Limey!" should do the trick.

Telephones: Orange.

Entertainment

Why did the British colonize so much? Because of the "white man's burden"—that is, because they **suck at sports**. The British are so unathletic that in order to ever *win* at anything, they had to make up their own sports—wimpy games like croquet and polo and badminton and cricket. Then, when no one would play with them, they were forced to travel all around the world setting up franchise teams to compete against. Once a colony started

---

[3]anal

beating them, the British granted them their independence.

In the "You know it's a tough game when everybody wears white and still has clean clothes at the end of the match" department is the British version of baseball,[4] called **cricket**, the object of which is to **bore your opponents into forfeiting the game**.

The interesting thing about cricket is that *nobody really understands how to play it*—not even the players. It has something to do with hitting a ball with an oar. That's all anyone knows. Cricket matches often go on for *days at a time* because neither side gets what's going on. Every once in a while someone will suggest a tea break, to which suggestion everyone nods vigorously and says "Yes, yes! Quoite!" The game stops for a few hours while they all rest up and repress their uniforms and try to figure out just exactly what's happening. Finally, after a few days of this, one team realizes it has better things to do with its time, such as **fox hunting** or **empire losing**, and forfeits.

 ## Understanding Those Peculiar Natives

Of all the unsolved mysteries in the British Isles—**Stonehenge, the Loch Ness Monster**, most **pub food**—perhaps none is stranger than the **British sense of humo(u)r**. Brits who can sit through entire Bugs Bunny marathons without a single snort will, when shown a film of *perfectly normal* British people doing *perfectly normal* British things,[5] bust out laughing like hogs in heat, afterwards saying things like "I was afraid I was going to lose my tea there for a moment."

If you're speaking with a Brit and you think he may have just said something which was supposed to be funny, just chuckle politely and murmur, "Oh, ho ho, so they say!" Even if he wasn't trying to be humorous, he'll still appreciate your thoughtfulness.

LONDON

London, also known as the Theatre District, is a city whose inhabitants have cheerfully learned to cope with the heavy tourist population by convincing them all to ride in big, red **double-decker buses** that always seem to go a little too fast around the curve next to the Thames.

---

[4]or Parcheesi
[5]rated G

BE BOLD! BE STUPID! BE AMERICAN!

Ask a guard, "When do we get to kiss the Rosetta Stone?"

Sights

London's most popular sight is **Westminster Abigail Van Buren**, home of the **World's Laziest Undertaker** who one day got bored and buried a bunch of famous people **right under the floor**. We just hope he wasn't in charge of the garbage as well.

And be sure to visit the **British Museum**, the country's most renowned collection of ancient objects.[6] Among its prized possessions are the **Rosetta Scone**, the ancient breakfast muffin which William the Irregular used to sink the entire Spanish Armada in 1215; the **Elgin Marbles**, located in back next to the **Elgin Jacks**, **Elgin Dominoes**, and **Elgin Game-Boy**; and an ancient copy of the **Magna Carta**, which became **Visa** in 1977.

Be sure to visit the **Leaning Tower of London**, where you can see on display the **Queen's Crown Jewels**. Ouch! Unfortunately, they're behind a **big glass panel**, so the closest you'll be able to get to them is to bang your fists against the window shouting "**Elaine! Elaine!**" This is a great trick to impress the guards with, and we've made special arrangements so that if you do this, they'll reward you by taking you to see something they called the **gaol**, which sounds very interesting, whatever it is.

Everyone should be sure to visit **Madame Toussaud's Wax Museum and Ear Cleaning Facility**. Here you'll see **frozen statues of Benny Hill**, a **Michael Jackson Through the Years** display, and the real **Al Gore**. Check out the **Chamber of Horrors** in the basement, also known as the museum café.

And what would a trip to London be without seeing **Big Ben?**[7] Be sure to visit this one—it's a "real looker." Well-read travelers know that Big Ben itself is neither the tower nor the clock. Big Ben is actually the **obese guard** at the bottom with the red suit and Marge-Simpson-hairdo-style hat who will **whack you on the head** if you try to get too close.

Tourists are not allowed on top of Big Ben. He is not a hobby-horse.

---

[6]runner-up: The Rolling Stones
[7]**answer:** a trip to London

Standing outside of **Buckingham Palace**, which you should be sure to visit, are **guards**, on whom you will immediately practice the Mature American Custom of trying to get them to move by making **fish faces** in front of them. Buckingham Palace is also where the **queen** resides when she's not performing her traditional royal duties, such as presiding over soccer riots or posting bail for various relatives.

Europe Close-Up: Royal Pains

Europeans have an interesting deal going with certain members of their families, who are usually chosen for their lack of good looks or mental health. In exchange for letting their every personal crisis from toe fungus on up be splashed on the front pages of tabloids, citizens pay these families enormous gobs of money, provide them with an army of fused-spine guards, and (!) let them get in free to any sports event they want so long as they sit in box seats and wave and occasionally wear the traditional garb of **red bathrobes** and **large Cuisinart attachments** on their heads. This is intended to demonstrate the incredible culture and sophistication of said country.

For example, the **British royal family** has long been upheld as a symbol of England's greatness. This particular symbol of England's greatness is now dealing with divorce, separations, nude photo scandals, fires, affairs, financial troubles, and hushy-hush tales of late-night, drug-induced Ouija board seances in the queen's chamber.

Things weren't always this royally screwed. After a long history of fat, jolly kings with names like Ethelred the Unready, whose only real faults were an overeager tendency to **behead their wives**, the royal family seemed to find stability under **Queen Elizabeth II**, named after the famous cruise ship.

But **Prince Charles**—whose Letterman grin, Perot ears, and vague resemblance to the **Cat in the Hat** should serve as a warning to inbreeders everywhere—was not so fortunate. Soon after he married **Princess Diana**, Chuck became known around the château as quite a philanderer (a fancy word meaning "stamp collector"). Di's icy stares in public were like a kick right in the crown jewels, and soon the Poor Little Rich Boy had to make a decision: keep on keeping on his mistress, or try to save the marriage—the ultimate **"do or Di" situation.**

Well, you can't accuse Chuck of thinking too much with his

brain, and the recent split has caused many British to lose faith in their royal family, much like the **Chappaquiddick** incident made us lose faith in ours.

It's been a bad few years indeed for our beloved queen. What with her heir all messed up, relatives doing the shimmy on the Riviera, and the death of Freddie Mercury, things may never be the same.

 The British tend to take their regal-life soap operas very seriously. It is possibly the only thing that they ever express uninhibited emotion about, so if you value your life, **DO NOT MAKE FUN OF THE QUEEN** while in England. We here at *Don't Go* won't be surprised if we find ourselves sharing a flat with Salman Rushdie in the near future, hostages to a worldwide death threat by all bowler-hatted Englishmen just for saying the future king of England looks like the Cat in the Hat. Frankly, we consider that a compliment.

Opening day: the biggest unforeseen problem with the Channel Tunnel

Culture

The British have this whiny, paranoid idea that nothing ever goes right for their country, one of the wealthiest in the world, and so they take every loss and setback—you know, they really have had quite a few—as proof that the world isn't fair. In order to cope with all these national embarrassments—and gosh, the more we think about them, there *have* been a lot—the British have become skilled masters of **denial**. The six stages of British recovery are denial, denial, denial, denial, denial, forgetting. We spent half an hour once trying to convince a young Brit that **Benny Hill really is dead**, and all he would do in response was look around and stutter nervously about what a damper the weather was today.

For denial is what the British do best, apart from ruining vegetables. They can take *any* unpleasant subject being discussed and ingeniously twist the conversation back to the **weather**, the *only topic* with which a Brit is entirely comfortable. For example:

Bad news: Wexford, your PARENTS and INNOCENT BABY SISTER have just been VAPORIZED by a NUCLEAR BOMB that went off in the MIDDLE OF LONDON!

Normal, appropriate response: WAAAAAAAAGHHHHH!!!!!!!

British response: Yes, well, hm. Well, I must say, well, I'm afraid I'm not terribly keen on this news, although we *were* rawther due for a spot of nawstiness as it were, although I must confess this is a bit out of the ord'nurry, even for this time of year. Hm, yes. Ahem. Rawther a bit of a damper, this weather, is it not?

BE BOLD! BE STUPID! BE AMERICAN!

In order to help the British overcome this denial, we suggest helping them to accept their most embarrassing failures—really, we can't believe how many there are! —whenever the opportunity arises. For example, say, "Well, you British certainly do have a lovely countryside, considering *not one* of your *four* soccer teams qualified for the World Cup. Isn't that funny, the U.S. will be playing while *you're not*, and we don't even *like* soccer! . . . Yes, a lovely countryside indeed."

Understanding Those Peculiar Natives

Many tourists choose to visit England because they've heard that English is spoken there. This is a common error. For example, we once asked a British friend of ours to translate the **real English** phrase "I was tired, so I took the elevator" into **British English**. Using standard British grammatical rules, this is the most concise translation:

> **I must bloody say bloody bloody that**
> **I was a bloody bit quoite bloody**
> **knackered, so I bloody procured the**
> **bloody lift. Ahem. Rawther a bit of a**
> **damper, this weather, is it not?**

Brits also have a cute habit of naming all their possessions. This helps them believe they still have some control over their surroundings.

CUTE LITTLE BRIT NAMES

NORMAL NAME	BRITISH NAME
policeman	Bobby
french fry	Chip
restroom	Lou
truck	Laurie
coattail-riding goofball	Ringo

You will notice once again the British denying the existence of anything troublesome—in this case, the **French**. It's not a french fry, it's a "chip"; and it's not french kissing, it's . . . Well, let's face it: the British don't *need* a word for that one.

OXFORD

Those ignorant, spiritually empty souls[8] who have never been to Oxford often have nothing more than a vague picture of a crusty old town filled with pretentious snots who do nothing but hold Latin debates, drink in pubs, and row, row, row.

---

[8]such as ourselves

If those souls were to spend any time at all in Oxford, they wouldn't hold this view at all. No, then they would have a very *clear* picture of a crusty old town filled with pretentious snots who do nothing but hold Latin debates, drink in pubs, and row, row, row.

Entertainment

Oxford is famous for its **pubs** with names like **Ye Olde Kit & Kaboodle** or **The Mangy Warthog's Trough**, whose main drink is **cider**. We have only one warning about this harmless-sounding beverage:

"This ain't no Mott's!"[9]

British students who even *think about* this stuff too strongly find themselves a few hours later lying semiconscious on the streets, resting in their own vomit, bemoaning the decline of their glorious empire, before—this is true—a **paddy wagon** comes by around midnight, scoops them up, and carts them all off.

Sometimes they make their way down to the river before expelling their cider, a pastime known to the students there as **punting into the Thames**.

Real Testimony: Oxford Row

We Americans have what you might call a superiority complex.[10] Or maybe not so complex; the philosophy doesn't usually get much deeper than "We're the best, and you guys suck."

This can peeve the British, who generally tend to lump American culture somewhere in between flavored popcorn and Menudo on the value to humanity scale. For example: We were at The Turf, an "authentic Oxford pub," which the locals recommend to all Americans so they don't go near the *real* authentic Oxford pubs. Here we met Luke, one of those **undernourished London punks**

---

[9]Copyright © Thank God for Harris! Enterprises. We are copyrighting this saying because we expect it to become a national craze, much like Rodney King's "Can we all get along?" Everybody will be saying "Hey! This ain't no Mott's!" to each other to the point that even **Jay Leno** will use it, whom we are **blatantly mentioning** so he'll invite us on **"The Tonight Show"** to promote this **book**. (Hint! Hint!)

[10]and rightly so

who are so skinny you could pitch horseshoes around them. When he started complaining about Americans' excessive patriotism, I naturally rose to the intellectual challenge:

"Well, that's 'cause we're the best and you guys suck."

"Oh, and wot geeves you sich in uppity attichyude?"

"Hey, man, the **U.S.A.** has made the world what it is today."

"Und you're sying you're proud o' that?"

"Hey, everything around you was invented by Americans. Cars. Airplanes. Television. The egg timer. The Clapper. Silly String . . ."

"The auto was invented by a Brit, y'know."

"Ah, that's okay. You guys are pretty much Americans."

"Hey, tyke that back! Wotch wot you say, you bastahd!"

"Please, when was the last time your president or prime minister or queenie-poo or whatever you call your leader now disagreed with U.S. policy?"

"Don't make fun of ahr queen."

"Thatcher left a drool stain on Reagan's suit every time they met. C'mon, aren't you guys a state yet? Oh, sorry, that's right— you're a *constitutional monarchy*. How very Lockean of you."

"Don't make fun of ahr queen."

"What, got a crush on her? Wanna get in on the inbreeding? Do some bucking in Buckingham? Perform the royal scam? How about—."

"AH SAID DON'T MAKE FUN OF AHR QUEEN!!" His eyes had a "Bill Bixby's about to get *really* angry" look, so I told him to chill out. "OK, but Americans did not invent evrythin' ahn this Earth."

"Well . . . Y'know the wheel? Yeah? . . . That was us, actually. And fire? It's 100 percent made in U.S.A."

"I haven't heard such a load of crap since I—"

"The opposable thumb? You can thank *good ol' Uncle Sam*."

"Yeah, well a whole lot o' good your opposable thumb is doing your country now. It's bloody fallin' apaht."

"You'd know."

"Us? Fallin' apaht? Perhaps me mate you hahve forgottin . . . *the Falkland War?*" The pub fell silent, mugs were stilled, and everyone started humming "My Country 'Tis of Thee" for some reason as Luke uttered those words of patriotism. The Falkland War was the **Official British Bright Spot in a Dismal Century**, a frenzied catfight in which England valiantly proved it could still hold its own against countries like Argentina. Sort of the Limey Grenada.

"Oh, sure. You're just still bitter about losing the *big* war."

"Wot do you mean, bitteh? We *won*. We were on the *same side*, you turd. You Americans really *do* suck at history."

"No, no. *The* war. The *Revolutionary War*, you scone head. Boy, did we tan your hides. What a slaughter. A blowout. A drubbing."

"Oh, the *Amicable Separation*, you mean? Some war. A bunch of drunks wearin' makeup dump their own tea over the side of a boat—Ah wouldn't exactly call that a blowout or whatever your baby word was."

"Baby word?"

"Yes, you Americans use such baby words. 'Oh, I go to school in California.' You don't bloody go to school. Twelve-year-olds go to school. You go to a univ*ahhh*sity. And what do you call those disgusting little orange cakes you've got, with the cream inside, that look like somebody's—."

"Twinkies?"

"Yes, 'Twinkies.' Whot a cute, baby name. And that thing that keeps a cahr quiet. Whot do you call it, a shusheh or shoosheh or something?"

"Muffler?"

"Oh yes, 'muffleh.' How cute. Just lahk what a baby would say. Goes along just dandy with your baby beers."

"Hey, don't mess with Old Milwaukee, man. . . ."

"You cahn't get pissed awff that crap."

"Pissed? Who said I was—oh, you mean *drunk*. What a cute *baby* word, Luke. But wait, I'm sorry. *Brits* don't have baby words. Oh, *nooo*. Only Americans. No baby words for Englishmen, no siree. And it's a jolly good pip-pip cheerio thing they don't, or else—hullo, what's this?—they'd bloody be bloody bloody ridiculed a whole bloody bloomin' lot, wouldn'tcha say, gov'nuh?"

"All royght, you Colonial, that's enough. Now Ah'm really peeved."

People were staring at us. I needed to reduce tensions. But how could I possibly get back on his good side and leave all our differences behind, reunite us in a common cause? Of course, there was only one solution.

"Now those **Frenchmen**, on the other hand . . ."

"*Ooooh*, those French! Bloody bastahds! Got their arrogant noses stuck in wine glasses. . . ."

"Land of the Brie, home of depraved, that's what I always say."

"Think they own the continent, think they're betteh than us. . . ."

"Yeah, sure, but how many *French* bases are there in the *U.S.*, huh?"

"Sittin' outside in their bloody cafés when it's sleeting and 10 below."

"Too bad they didn't show that kind of endurance during World War II, huh?"

"Yeah, bloody Maginot Lines. Brill. Just brill."

"More like i-maginary lines, huh? Some world power. Nice token seat on the UN Security Council. . . ."

"Bloody be speakin' *Doytch* if it weren't fer us. . . ."

We departed on the best of terms.

"Cheerio!"

"Wheatie!"

Accommodations

Old, One-Eyed Mother Thompkin's Bed & Breakfast: The classic B&B. Dotty old Mrs. Thompkin will patter on for hours in some incomprehensible dialect, showing you her rabid cat collection and discussing secret cooking tips ("Boil everything, Luv!"). Hours of feral enjoyment for the whole family. Go easy on the Feline Stew at dinner. Singles, £25. Doubles, £35. Canadian doubles, £40.

YMCA: It's fun to stay at. It's fun to play at. They've got everything that you need and more. They've got whatever you are looking for.

STONEHENGE

Stonehenge is an ancient and mysterious group of large stones aligned with astounding mathematical precision to resemble a **heap of neglected ruins**. What baffles scientists is that Stonehenge was built over 2,000 years ago, *before ruins even existed!*

Responsible for these king-sized building blocks are the **Druids**, an ancient group of Celts whose name means "morons." The Druids & Friends lugged these stones from hundreds of miles away to erect them here, only to abandon their project when they couldn't secure the proper building permits.

You may be most familiar with Stonehenge through those commercials for the ***Time/Life Series on Weird Shit***. You know,

> **A woman burns her hand on a griddle.**
> **Three thousand miles away, her mother**
> **buys replacement filters for the vacuum**
> **cleaner. *Coincidence?***

The one for Stonehenge went something like this:

> **A man bends a coat hanger into an ancient**
> **Egyptian symbol and points it at the center**
> **of Stonehenge. A burst of energy knocks**
> **him to the ground. *Coincidence?***

Now, we here at *Don't Go* think that the *real* mystery is why some ninny would take a bent coat hanger and point it at a pile of rocks to begin with. Was this a habit of his? Did he go around to other monuments before this without success—maybe waving a pipe cleaner shaped like an ampersand at the Louvre, or perhaps standing in front of the Roman Colosseum holding up a potato that resembled Milton Berle?

THE QUAINT, ROLLING COUNTRYSIDE

England is brewing with quaint, old-fashioned, city-state villages with quaint, old-fashioned names like **Bunionbury** and **Crazyches-ter** and **Onceford-upon-Atimekin**. Each one boasts a unique **single-event history**, detailed with much fanfare in its quaint, old-fashioned **multilingual tourist brochures**:

> In 1543, the city of Doop was attacked
> by a horde of evil sloth-riding Nougatians
> from the Northumberlands. The Doopan
> army, led by the bold young Weebert, was
> severely outnumbered. As legend has it,
> however, Weebert craftily snuck behind
> enemy lines and dumped yeast into the
> sloths' dinner. Under the hot sun in the
> next day's battle, the yeast expanded,
> causing the Nougatian sloths to explode
> underneath their hapless riders. In this

manner, the Doopans successfully repelled
the Nougatian invasion and preserved their
independence until falling to a small
Germanic kingdom three weeks later.

In celebration of this event, every year
on the anniversary of the invasion, people
in Doop hold the Weebert Festival, during
which citizens bake bread and then gamely
attempt to slide it under people's feet in
mock reenactment of the great battle.

Feel free to participate in the
gay festivities!

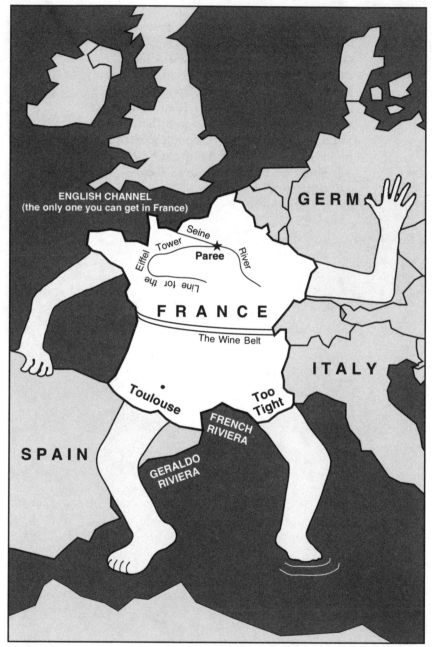

Geographic Irony: The nation of France resembles a clean pair of underwear.

France
Land of the French

How we miss the land of passion—
Wondrous food and wild romance,
Rustic lands, exotic fashion!
Boy, we're homesick here in France.

FRANCE
VITAL INFORMATION

Currency in use: The baguette

Dominant stereotype: Sissy, croissant-eating, pasty-faced frogs with no butts

Official motto: *Itus nottum E. ze being greenus*

Theme song: "We Are the Champignons"

For fun: Leapfrogging, Jerry Lewis telethons

Contributions to American culture: French fries, french bread pizzas, French's mustard, Pépé le Pew

Ugly American visits, returns with: Little plastic Eiffel Tower, fashionable purple bidet on the head,[1] Wonder Bread withdrawal

Rating (−10 to 0): −11

How to sound like you've really, truly been there: "Uh! The *Mona Lisa* was so much *smaller* than I expected!"

So. Is it all baguettes and berets? Whining and dining? Accents and asses? Is France truly the land of the Brie, home of depraved?

Why, butt*uvcals*! This is Weenieworld, Le Le Land, Pansies with Pastries, a defensively snotty region where the slightest public mention of American culture will send a native flying into a state known as **the French Conniption**.

Sure, the Riviera may *sound* nice and all, until you factor in a hundred thousand elitist natives trying to **spit on you** who consider their oodles of poodles more cultured than any American. So skip it. Forget France. After all, you know the saying, "With French like these, who needs any **Nice**?"

History
For over two millenia, France has firmly and valiantly held its ground as a second-rate power that gets its little Dijonnaise butt whupped almost every time it goes to war.

---

[1]A purple *beret.* Sorry.

PRESENTING A QUICK AND PAINFUL LOOK AT FRANCE'S WAR RECORD

DATE	VS.	HOME/ AWAY	STATS	RESULTS
58–51 B.C.	Romans	H	Got whupped, diced, shellacked, and occupied	L
771–814	Barbarians	A	(Charlemagne) Conquered Europe, then bit it	W
1337–1453	England	H	(Hundred Years' War) Squeaked by with win in extra innings	W
1667–1714	Invitational		Louis "Steinbrenner" XIV bankrupts country, paving way for disastrous slump that follows	W, T, L, L
1765–1768	England	A	Another pummeling— this time here in the Americas (woo woo!)	L
1800–1815	Europe	A	(Napoleon*) See Charlemagne	T

(continued on the next page)

---

*Napoleon was known to his subordinates as "one helluva SHOGWA (Short Guy With an Attitude)." The Napster's theme song was "Elba Room" ("Elba room, Elba room, got to book me one of them Elba rooms").

DATE	VS.	HOME/ AWAY	STATS	RESULTS
1870	Prussians	H	Two-month-long "in your face" debacle kicks off winless streak vs. new archrival	L
1914–1918	Germans	H	Bogged down in the Whineland—had to be bailed out by us Americans	T
1940–1944	Germans	H	Got whupped, diced, shellacked, and occupied—had to be bailed out by us Americans	L
1950–1954	Vietnamese	A	Got out before getting whupped, diced, and shellacked— had to be bailed out by us Americans (Oops)	Forfeit

Total record: 3–7–3

Winless for over **300 years**? C'mon, even **Bangladesh** had a victory in '71. The French military couldn't threaten even **Luxembourg** these days, let alone a *real* country—what'll they do if we make them mad, throw espressos on us?

In modern times, France has pioneered new and exciting ways of losing. For example: the French want to stop **those nutty Germans** from barreling down into their country every time they've had a few to many *biers* and feel like they could conquer the world.

So how does one tie down those type A Deutschlanders? Why, create the **European Community**, so that the two countries would join economic forces. This clever trick has assured that, assuming their economic growth trends continue, the Germans will never invade France because they'll own most of the country anyway.

 You may also notice from the chart that the French owe us Americans so much that you'd think they wouldn't be such rude hosts when we decide to drop by. We've fought three of their wars for them, liberated their country twice, and even patted them on the head and said all right when they asked for a seat on the UN Security Council, and the only thing that *we've* gotten out of any Franco-American alliance is **SpaghettiOs**.

 ### Practical Information
Normal man may not live on bread alone, but the French-man, remember, is not a normal man.[2] **Bread** and **water**, unlike other food in France, is cheap, simple, was never heard to say "ribbit," and doesn't require paying some skinny-ninny waiter a non-negotiable 15 percent tip for bringing it to you more slowly than it would have taken had you just sat around and waited for the effects of **continental drift**. So if you have plans to eat in France, we say just "baguette" and listen to the sound of logic: Don't get mad; get Evian.

Understanding Those Peculiar Natives
Because it is such a rare commodity within their own coun-try, the French respond eagerly when rewarded with *common courtesy*. This includes **rule number *un* for getting along with**

---

[2]He may, however, be a normal woman.

those French weenies, which should be committed to memory and never forgotten when speaking with the French:

Don't bring up the Second World War.

The other thing you must do is to **always try to speak in French before resorting to English.** Even if you speak *no French*, you should still wave your arms around a little and go "Eu ... eu ..." through your nose before launching into the standard "Yee-ha! Yee-ha! Anglais! Anglais!" This is to give the deluded Frenchpeople a false sense of security that folks in the rest of the world still give a turnip about learning their dead language.

Following are the most important phrases you will need in France:

● **"Er, excuse me, but your adorable midget dog has just made poo-poo all over my sneakers."** *Eu, pardonnez-moi, mais votre petit chien adorable vient de faire le poo-poo partout mes chaussures.*

● **"Ah, yes, wasn't that during the reign of Louis?"** *Ah oui, c'était pendant le règne de Louis, n'est-ce pas?*

● **"Sacred blue! You have such a beautiful country!"** *Sacrebleu! Vous avez un si grand nez!*

● **"To start, I would like to pay a lot of money for some slugs in garlic sauce."** *Des escargots, s'il vous plaît.*

● **"Hey, where's French Disneyland?"** *Hé, où est le Disneyland Français?*

● **"Buzz off, you beret-wearing, coffee-drinking Eurofreak."** *Buzzez-vous fermé, vous béret-portant, café-buvant Eurofreaque.*

 And remember, a **beret** is what you wear on your head; a **bidet** is what you wash your butt in. Never, *ever* put a bidet on your head, and whatever you do, *don't* use a beret to wash your butt.

Transportation
Le TGV (the TGV) is an abbreviation for France's pride and joy, *le Train* à *Grande Vitesse* (the Train at Big Fetus), a system of really, really, really, really, really fast trains in France that don't very often derail. So if you—oops, did we mention derailing? How silly of us! The TGV is *safe, perfectly safe*, and has never as far as we know exploded into a

FIREBALL OF DEATH

with **passengers screaming** and **twisted metal flying everywhere**. Safe, safe, safe. Yesiree. The TGV's motto should be "Ride with us, and *ne worry-vous pas* about becoming a mangled chunk of bloody charcoal!" And we would believe it. That's why we never give a second thought about the safety of TGV passengers while crossing France in our **rented car**.

THE RIVIERA

Older Americans have **Florida**; older French have . . . well, they have a lot of hair in their ears, but they also have the Riviera, their own mecca for the retired and toothless. Known as **le Côte d'Azur**, it tries to seem like a young, raging city, but we can't help but get the same uncomfortable feeling there that we did watching **George Bush** appear on **MTV**. The French may think it's the "Gaul of the wild," but it looks more like the set of *Cocoon* to us.

 ### Europe Close-Up: European Dogs
Europeans *loooove* dogs. Now that our cross-Atlantic cronies have lost all their colonies and these days can't claim mastery over anything bigger than the coffee bean, they've resorted to hanging out with man's best friend in order to still feel superior.

So they allow dogs everywhere in Europe: eating off plates in **restaurants**, riding the **subway**, drooling in **supermarkets**, or just hanging out in **bars**, sometimes with their owners.

Nowhere is the dog glut worse than in southern France, where you'll find the elusive

RAT-DOGS of the RIVIERA.

For, like its monuments, countries, bathing suits, supermarkets, ice cream portions, and trade deficit, Europe's pint-sized, punt-sized dogs are **granola dust** compared to our big BIG **BIG** American kind.

Sure, European apartments could make a sardine can look like Montana, but that's no excuse for attaching leashes to **long-eared squirrels**. These half-sized canines (cafours?) hardly reach to the knee. This *does* make them easier to **kick** when the owners aren't looking, but why don't they just get cats?

Maybe it's sympathy that gets **rich Rivieran widows** to buy them. Or maybe it's just the French infatuation with **losers** coming through. Who cares? Foot-long dogs belong in ball parks, not on the streets.

The favorite companion for the rich Rivieran widow is the **poodle**.[3] The women shave these poor poodles into strange shapes, tie poodle ribbons in their hair, spray poodle perfume on them, take them to poodle hairdressers and poodle shrinks and poodle manicurists and poodle masseuses, and do whatever else they can to make them look as perfectly revolting as possible. Ideally, Fifi will end up looking exactly like her owner, only not the size of a small automobile.

So down the boulevard Fifi and owner stroll, leaving nothing but sweet-smelling, dainty plops of poodle poop behind them.

 Lamb, Lamb, Lamb: Fun With Poodles!
If you get some free time in the Riviera, grab a friend and enjoy the innocent pursuit of finding out how many dog owners know English. Walking a few paces behind, avoiding the poodle puddles and poodle piddles around you, try out the following passing comments on wealthy widows.

"*See?* I told you. If you put your dog in the dryer for too long, it'll *shrink*, and its *hair* will *bunch up*, and—Oh my gosh, it's lost control over its bowels! *Look out!*"

"Good gravy! Europe is so civilized, they even keep their **rats** on leashes!"

"Man, that's the most symmetrical mange I've ever seen."

"Just look at it—perfect aerodynamic dimensions. I could launch it a good 50 yards, with the wind."

---

[3] named Fifi

BE BOLD! BE STUPID! BE AMERICAN!

If you ever run into a Frenchperson giving
commands to her dog, walk up with a look of shock
on your face and say, "Wow! I can't be*lieve* that your dog
can understand *FRENCH!*"

Cannes

The sun is shining, the beaches are nudist, and the water is a
beautiful 2000 Flushes shade of blue, so naturally everyone in
Cannes stays inside and watches movies. During **April's festival**,
crowds swarm to watch films compete in such categories as
Most Boring, Self-Indulgent Autobiographical Work by a European Director, Film the Fewest People Have Ever Heard Of, and
Longest Title.[4]

 Don't Go! Tickets are impossible to
get for anyone who cannot prove
that he's either a director or Arnold
Schwarzenegger. And groupies are
discouraged with impressive thoroughness by
large bouncers named Vinny. So you can go
ahead and try a **star trek**, but all you'll end
up getting is the **wrath of Cannes**.

Saint-Tropez

Pronounced "SAN-TRO-PAY, PAY, PAY!" 'Nuff said.

Nice

You don't *really* expect us here at *Don't Go* to say Nice is nice, do
you? You don't *really* think so little of this guidebook that you

---

[4]last year's winner: *La Kartenspiel de la Palazzi Bohème Con Carné* Σγψοθων
Mea Culpa in Red Part III: Nikita Lives

suppose we'd stoop that low now, huh? Besides, it's pronounced "nees," you Neanderthal.

If we *were* to make a joke about this city's name—and we are not, mind you—then it would be this:

> **I spent six days in this town,**
> **but that's all I could handle; I guess I was**
> **getting a little *week in the Nice*.**

But what we're trying to tell you is, we wouldn't say that.

PARIS

Ah, Paris . . . Great city.
My one mistake was to put it in France.
—God

Paris is a Harvard *Let's Go: Europe* writer's dream city. No other place can handle so many academic Latin words in its description without sounding like Catholic mass at the Mensa institute. For example, take "Paris slakes the human **thirst for perfection**."

Slakes? What is *slakes*? If you mean *quench*, say "quench." And do humans truly *thirst* for perfection? Wouldn't most of us settle for a cold beer? But keep reading: "If Paris did not exist, we would have to invent it. If we did not exist, **Paris wouldn't care**."

ANGST! ANNNNNNNNGST! Quick, get us an espresso and set us down with Hemingway before we revert to the meaningless, Coke-drinking shells of Americans that we truly are!

But wait, there's more! The fourth sentence reads: "Paris remains no less than the **nucleus of human civilization**, an incarnation of the mythological longing for luxury, indulgence, romance, and beauty."

Like, gag us with a sorbet spoon.

In her *very first* paragraph about Paris, *Let's Go* writer "Horrible Hannah" Feldman uses *eight* words over three syllables long, tosses out *seven* references to literary figures, and still finds room for such flowery phrases as "allegorical contentment," "heartbreaking beauty," and the ever-popular "nostalgic longing."

That's the danger of using Harvard students to write your travel guides. You end up with a rambling discourse on the intellectual-historical impact of a city instead of just a list of cool things to see and steal.

Practical Information
Paris is split by the Seine River into *la Rive Droite* (the Right Bank) and *la Rive Gauche* (the Crude Bank). The river itself, like all water in Europe, is **totally grody**, and anyone who swims in it has clearly gone in Seine.

The Left Bank was supposedly once full of pretentious, bidet-wearing, student/philosopher–king types.[5] Now it's a bunch of touristy cafés with signs outside that boast—in English—ERNEST HEMINGWAY DRANK HERE.

Listen, bubs, Ernest Hemingway drank *everywhere*. The focus of the Left Bank is on *left*, as in leftist music, leftist politics, and exploiting anything that's left over from its glory days.

The focus of the **Right Bank**, on the other hand, is on **bank**, as in "You'll need to make many trips to the bank to survive here." *This* is the Paris we know and despise.

Transportation
European **subways** will give you a bit of culture shock the first time you ride them because you will probably not get **mugged**. Riding Paris's subway is particularly efficient, for you avoid all the automobiles driving on the city's roads, streets, and sidewalks.

Furthermore, we at *Don't Go* have discovered that driving in Paris is a lot tougher than you might think. For example, we took a cab from the train station to our hotel, and in order to get there, it was necessary to drive by the train station *three different times*. And even though on a map the hotel *seemed* like it was just a few blocks down a main road, we actually had to take numerous long, winding back streets to get there. But the **cab driver** was extremely patient throughout, and we made certain to give him a **large tip**.

Food
France has found a unique way of controlling its unwanted critter population. They have done this by giving animals like **snails**, **pigeons**, and **frogs** fancy names, thus transforming common backyard pests into expensive delicacies. These are then served to gullible tourists, who will eat anything they can't pro-

---

[5] *Beret*-wearing. Sorry.

nounce; the French could serve *la wadde du gum à la sidewalk* and folks would still gobble it up.

The worst abuse of the "expensive name makes an expensive dish" trick is the **pâté de foie gras**, or liver pâté, which is a delicately prepared, exquisitely garnished, **mushed-up pile of liverwurst**.

Other foods to avoid eating are **frogs' legs**, which as far as we're concerned amounts to **cannibalism** in France, and something called **aspic**, the pronunciation of which alone was enough to scare us away.

Europe Close-Up: A Bottle of Red

The only way us barbaric, Coke-slurping Americans can grasp the importance of selecting the proper wine is, one Frenchman told us, to compare it to whatever is the most important selection process in *our* culture. So, think of the wine list as a preseason roster of **NFL teams**, and think of choosing a wine as figuring out which team you should put money on to win the **Super Bowl**.

Groups of old men will spend *hours* before each meal loudly debating the strengths, weaknesses and past records of each wine, outdoing each other with useless stats.[6] Now everyone has a home-town favorite, and some harsh insults invariably fly out about how the Besançon burgundies couldn't hold their own against a bucket of horse urine, but in the end, some agreement is made.

Next comes the taste test. The **wine guy** brings out the bottle, shows the label to the nodding crowd, and opens it up. Each old man sniffs the cork as it's passed around, making a pleasant comment such as, "Ah, yes, a very fine cork, indeed."

Next, about three molecules of the wine are poured into a glass. The elected taster stares at it for a while, comments on the color, swishes it around, comments on the swishiness, and then raises the glass to his nose.

His nose, at this point, actually stretches down *into* the glass and begins poking around the inside, testing every cubic millimeter for its "bouquet." After this, the nose resurfaces, returns like Stretch Armstrong to its original shape, and exhales. The taster then makes a pleasant comment about the smell, such as "Ah, yes, a very fine smell, indeed."

Finally, he takes a small sip, smacks his lips a few times, knots

---

[6]"Hey Normie, it's a little-known fact that the Haut-Briand Bordeaux of an even-numbered year when the frost came early has never been a smart pick when matched with steak."

his eyebrows and with a vigorous, as-if-overcoming-constipation nod annouces, "BON!"

Party time! They won the Super Bowl! *Passez-vous les beer nuts!* The onlookers break into smiles, congratulating each other on their own impeccable taste. At this point, everyone gets into the act: "Fine bouquet," "A playful yet didactic aroma," "Smooth, yet spritely," "Self-adhesive, yet not overtly isosceles," "It springs forth from the confines of the glass in a voluptuous manner, its bosom heaving, and yet, just when you expect it to embrace you passionately in its full body, it draws back, teasing you, saying, 'No, let's talk first,' until you are heartbroken, distressed, and ready to swallow it all and move on. It is then, at your lowest moment of despair, that it suddenly comes around and fills you with its overwhelming fragrance, making the reunion all that much sweeter," "Red . . . but kinda whitish too."

May we recommend the **'94 Coke**?

BE BOLD! BE STUPID! BE AMERICAN!

Five words: "Is the wine here fresh?"

 ## Europe Close-Up: The Hardest Part

The great thing about French restauarants is that there's never any doubt who the waiter is—**you are**. You'll do more waiting in a French restaurant than in Hell's post office, and for two reasons:

1. French law requires that meals be split into about **39 different courses**, from *apéritif* to *toothpique*. Patrons of the fanciest restaurants can spend entire weekends at their table before even seeing the dessert menu. Personally, we'd gladly give up a few *sorbets* if it meant not getting such *sorebutts*.

2. Everything in Paris must be **fresh**—not just the **men**. Cooks want you to think everything's made from scratch, even if "scratch" really just refers to their method for removing the microwaveable wrapper. If you order meat, they'll make you wait at least as long as it would take to slaughter, skin, chop, pickle, and cook the animal. If you complain that your bread is taking too long, the waiter will calmly assure you that "the wheat is being sown right this moment, Madam."

When ordering meats in Europe, one should be aware of the slight difference in cooking times that Europeans use.

IF YOU ORDER YOUR MEAT	THEN YOU'LL GET IT
well done	medium-rare
medium-well	rare
medium	bloody, ass-kickin' rare
medium-rare	"tartare, me maties!"
rare	alive 'n' mooing, with a side order of hatchet

After you've eaten a fancy meal, to celebrate the new day, the **cheese guy** will come around and ask if you would like to sample any number of moldy, melted cheeses that have been lovingly displayed for the past week on the shelf under a warm plastic lid. Not only are some of them not Day-Glo orange like any good cheese should be, but *the portions are not individually wrapped.* "If it didn't come out of a squeeze bottle, it's not the cheese for us!" These are words to live by. We suggest ordering another **Coke** instead.

Real Testimony: Whining and Dining

Mike and I took our seats. After telling the wine guy which expensive wine we wanted to be charged for while they actually served us the French equivalent of grape Snapple, I looked at the menu. Rather than sacrificing my manhood by asking someone to translate for me,[7] I just picked some clever-sounding dish whose meaning I couldn't figure out.

I was bold. I was daring. I had the foresight of a Fudgsicle. For all I knew, I could have ordered Roast Filet of Cute Poodle or, in an absolute worst-case scenario, the German Sausage Sampler. Actually, that would have been preferable to what I ordered, which was a dish called *le Rognon Bouilli.*

The waiter, who had obviously taken an **English for Smart-Asses** course, raised his eyebrows and winked at me. "Soooo, you like *le Rognon Bouilli?*"

---

[7]This is a symptom of the same brain dysfunction common to all "real men" which prevents a male from ever stopping at a gas station for directions, even if he's three days late and road signs suggest that he may be on the wrong continent.

My head bounced up and down a few times. "Oh, *oui, oui*," I grinned nervously. "*Très, très* much."

The next day, the waiter brought out our entrees, presenting me with a dark purplish, jiggling blob. "Yuck!" I said, trying to conceal my disgust. "That looks like a . . . I don't know, a *boiled kidney!*"

The waiter spoke only one terrible, awful word in reply: "But-tuv*cals!*"

After the *Psycho* music faded, I regained my composure, cut up the kidney, and managed in time to swallow every bite of it, grinning and waving sickly at the waiter while he snickered into the curtains across the room.

 The differences in the "proper" European and American styles of holding utensils and eating meat are important to know. For the average, right-handed diner:

Proper European method: With one's *left hand*, gently push the fork, tines facing *downward*, into a corner of the meat. Holding the knife in one's *right hand*, carefully cut away that portion of the meat. One should then be able to bring the meat up to one's mouth in a single, refined, educated, upper-class, elitist stroke *without* having the fork switch hands. Repeat.

Proper American method: Place meat firmly between two sesame seed buns, pour on ketchup and canned cheese product, and rip bites off with teeth.

Entertainment

No one travel guide could ever do justice to **Paris at night**. So, **we won't even try**. Besides, we here at *Don't Go* were having kidney problems that night, and nothing looked more appealing than our **hotel bed**, which was a first, since it was so soft that whenever we climbed into it we sank approximately **two stories**.

However, we can recommend some excellent **dubbed American television shows,**[8] if you're interested.

Sights

The **Cathédrale de Notre Dame** is a big church that one researcher described as a good place in which to **make out**, although we personally feel she is going to **burn in hell for eternity** for that. The outside's cute too—steeples, stained-glass windows, stone replicas of **Kiss band members** sitting on the walls—but watch out for those **flying buttresses**.

A few famous bridges and *la Place de*s away is the **Louvre**. This art museum has one of the **biggest collections in the world**, although it may as well be a **fertilizer plant** because all *you're* going to do there is rush in, snap a pic of the *Mona Lisa*, and rush out. Better bring your zoom lens: ol' Mona is possibly the most expensive **postage stamp** in the world.

DON'T GO'S TOP EIGHT
MOST POPULAR ATTRACTIONS IN THE LOUVRE*

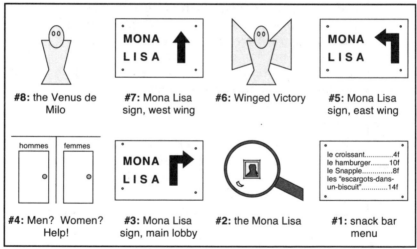

*Rankings are based on the average time Americans spend in front of each.

What do you get when you cross Greek art with *Boxing Helena*? Why, the **Venus de Milo**, which you can tell apart from all the *other* quadriplegic statues around because . . . because . . . well,

---

[8]"CHiPs," anyone?

because there's a big crowd around it. Old art, broken sculptures, and *no dinosaur bones*. While in Paris you can Louvre it or leave it, as far as we're concerned.

Napoleon commissioned hundreds of men to build the **Arc de Triomphe** in honor of his army, and then proceeded to meet his Waterloo (literally), so you may also refer to it as the **Arc de Whoops We Spoke Too Soon**. One gets the feeling that maybe if the French had spent a little less time and effort building arches of triumph for themselves, they might have won a few more wars. Underneath is the **Tomb of the Unknown Soldier**, where a Name This Soldier contest is still going on, so put your ideas in the box nearby.[9]

Also at the Arc is the **eternal flame**, immortalized in the song by the **Bangles**. According to *Let's Go*, the eternal flame is rekindled every evening at 6:30 P.M.

Huh?

Last is the **Eiffel Tower**, the largest structure ever created with an erector set and once thought by Parisians to be pretty damn ugly.

Stare at it long enough, and you will soon discover **the secret of the Eiffel Tower**. "You know . . . this thing really is **pretty damn ugly.**"

Culture

Parisian culture is centered around little cups of concentrated caffeine that tourists all love to drink while snottily complaining about "all 'em damn t'rists around here."

> Parisian elitism is contagious. No one ever considers *themselves* to be a tourist in Paris. But anyone who's been in Paris *less* time than you is automatically an immature, intruding bonehead. For example, if you get in on the 3:30 train, and your companion comes in on the 4:25, you will for the rest of your visit treat him like he's an evolutionary step below Enos from "The Dukes of Hazzard."

---

[9]May we suggest Skip?

Europe Close-Up: Cafés

Other countries may have their own versions of the café (Germany: **das Café**; Spain: **café olé**), but only the French reach that perfect blend of freezing outdoor patios, $6 drinks, and waiters who appear about once every third Tuesday that makes the café what it is.[10]

The first-time visitor may be overawed by the selections of coffee available, but the general rule is **the more expensive a drink, the less coffee there actually is.** At the ritziest places, the most expensive and popular beverage is *un café rien*, which is a very small cup with **absolutely nothing** in it.

But we wouldn't say that *all* the people in Paris cafés are tourists, or else we'd be forgetting the **pompous *artiste*-Euro-freaks.** They sit outside in the latest fashion,[11] staring at passersby until one (hopefully, a tall American woman) returns what may in some parallel universe be considered a suggestive gaze.

At this point, the *artiste* rushes up to the American, and the standard conversation ensues:

Art Monger: You ahre *magnifique*. Ah wood lahk to pent you. Will you let me pent you?

American Woman: Um, let me see here. . . . [flipping through her guidebook] Buzzez-vous fermé, vous beret-portant, café-buvant Eurofreaque.

 ## Europe Close-Up: Le Café

The exact origins of coffee remain uncertain, if only because it's difficult to imagine the thought processes of the first herdsman to concoct the beverage: "Pffft! Blech, this stuff is awful! But I'm sure that if I keep drinking it every day, I'll **acquire the taste.**" Nonetheless, for fifteen hundred years, coffee has been solidifying its jittery hold on Europeans. This[12] probably explains the large number of wars that Europe has had over the ages: You'd be a bit edgy too if you had that much caffeine in your system.

---

[10]a colossal waste of time
[11]When we visited, the latest fashion was anything with (Woo woo!) American writing on it, so you'd see smooth dudes wearing leather jackets with things like "American baseball" written on them. Coolness!
[12]along with the Germans

Lamb, Lamb, Lamb: Euro Disney

Euro Disney is one of the greatest places to go if you accidentally find yourself in Europe, because it's almost *exactly the same as Disneyland in the U.S.* That is, it's the same except it's empty. If you do see anyone else, they'll all be **shallow Americans who've traveled all the way to Europe just to hang out in an American theme park**. So if you hide out here for the whole trip, it'll be like you never left home! Bonus! Or, as they say in France, *nus de bo*!

However, so the slight changes don't catch you off guard, review this list:

DON'T GO'S TOP TEN WAYS
EURO DISNEY IS DIFFERENT

10. Main Street U.S.A. touted as a horror ride.

9. Minnie Mouse is topless.

8. Antiforeigner graffiti outside It's a Small World After All.

7. Swiss Family Robinson Treehouse voted to stay separate from the rest of the park.

6. Most popular snack: Mr. Toad's Wild Legs.

5. Hall of Presidents and Flying Dumbos combined into one attraction.

4. The Matterhorn really *is* the Matterhorn.

3. Bonus attraction: Russian World, a long snaking line with nothing at the end of it.

2. 96,540 Kilometers Under the Sea.

1. EPCOT's World Showcase pavilions really just exit on different sides of the park.

THE REST OF FRANCE

The Rest of France is a beautiful little village nestled among the rolling hills of the wine country, filled with good-natured **French-people** who will be more than happy to invite you into their homes to discuss France in their native tongue while they tend the **vineyards** or perform the ritual **autumn harvesting of their nostril hairs**. Unfortunately, in order to preserve this pastoral scene, the Rest of France is also **closed to Americans**. Sorry.

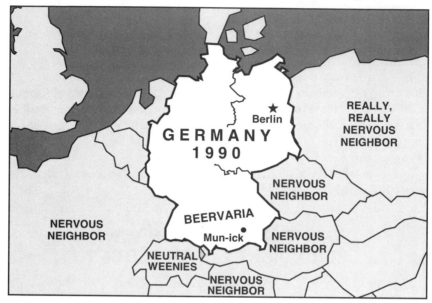

German View: Unification 1990 = a good start

World View: Unification 1990 = a good scare

Ultra Mongo-Huge Reunified Chapter
Not East Germany...
Not West Germany...
but
Germany!

Waiting on the corner, yes,
Until the light says "walk." What patience!
Standing there, who'd ever guess
Their love for staging mass invasions?

GERMANY
VITAL INFORMATION

Currency in use: The Mark[1]

Dominant stereotype: Blond-haired, beer-guzzling, overweight, xenophobic, square-jawed robot doberman police

Official motto: "Das bigger, das better"

Theme song: "Ve Are Der Vorld"

For fun: "Hey, let's all go see what Poland is up to!"

Contributions to American culture: "Sprockets," *The Love Bug*, *Casablanca*'s storyline

Ugly American visits, returns with: Silly feathered Bavarian hat, chunk of sidewalk with "official piece of the Berlin Wall" tag, one ultra mongo-huge hangover

Overall rating (−10 to 0): −6

How to sound like you've really, truly been there: "Uh! I'll never be able to drink these *American* beers again!"

Germans are just plain nutty. First of all, they live in this big, sausage-grinder-shaped country. Everything's real big: words, waistlines, plans for future growth (say as far as **New Zealand**). But then again, whaddya expect from a country that's perpetually in the German-nation stage?

Also, they live in a diverse *Pot von Melting* in which such different peoples as **whites**, **heterosexuals**, **Protestants**, and **males** all coexist in peace, love and bratwurst.

German nuttiness is a **documented fact**—they *love* to get out **und boogie**, as they often say. Check out these fruit-loopy factoids

---

[1]As do the money unit terms Franc and Buck, the Mark further proves that wealth is unfairly considered a male trait in Western society. Does any country use the Hilda? The Janet? The Patricia? No, the sexist pigs.

that you'd never think would apply to Everyone's Favorite Master Race:

- Thanks to their $2.795 \times 10^{3,986}$ varieties of beer, Germany is the only place in the world where you can get drunk on a train and wake up in the middle of a Hannover. Never doubt that Germans play a very "imported" role in American entertainment.

- **Those nutty Germans**, knowing when they have a good thing going, actually have *two* cities named Frankfurt.[2]

- During the last years of the '80s, the highest-rated American import TV show was "Alf." Now *that's* culture!
Alf is probably the only **alien** that Germans have *ever* willingly let into their country. This is not to say that they object to new citizens. It's just that over the years their policy has been **"Don't come to us; we'll come to you."**

- Finally, the way they dot their vowels, we'd swear they're doing it to make **cute, pooky, little smiley faces** out of their letters: ü
Now aren't you surprised? ö

History

Germans first made their Deutschmark on history about 2,000 years ago, when hordes of **Germanic barbarians** went roaring across Europe looking for free beer. Since then, however, Germans have become *much* more civilized, and only **twice in this entire century** have they tried anything like world domination again.

Not until the 1800s did a big German state arise, called **Prussia**, a name that is sort of a cross between "Russia" and ... the letter *P.* Prussia and Russia teamed up to conquer **Poland**, which is sort of like **Sylvester Stallone** enlisting the aid of **Jean-Claude Van Damme** to remove a mildew stain. Poland collapsed like a bleacher at an English soccer match. (They just couldn't take the Prussia, we guess.) By the end of the century, the rest of Germany had been unified under **Bismarck**, a man strong and iron-willed despite his being named after the **capital of North Dakota**.

In 1914 the Germans, infected by that age-old *Wanderlust*,[3] decided it was time to get out and conquer the world a little. **France**

---

[2]Frankfurt and the lesser-known Frankfurt.
[3]or maybe it was the quest for a decent meal

was the logical warm-up country. So they invaded the Whineland, only to be stopped cold after a month by hordes of fashion-conscious Frenchies who'd come to laugh at the Germans' "pointy leetle helmets."

Next came **Hitler**, the most universally hated man of all time next to that guitar player on "Saturday Night Live." Hitler's psychological problems should have been clear from the start because he seems to always have missed the *same exact spot* when shaving. Cleverly disguising himself as **Charlie Chaplin**, Hitler infiltrated the government and soon put into place his **diabolical scheme** which involved making everyone else walk around the streets with one arm sticking up in the air, thus torturing his first ethnic group, **cab drivers**. This was the infamous "hail a taxi" initiative. Unfortunately, some inexperienced temp mistyped it as "heil a nazi," and that's when the trouble *really* started.

Blinded by racism (hence, the **Not-See Party**), putting the *manic* back in "Germanic," Hitler's forces beer-barreled through the rest of Europe, and only the good ol' **U.S.A.** was there to save the continent,[4] although sometimes we wonder about that decision.

To make sure that Germany never again took over Europe, the U.S. and Soviet Union together took two precautions:

1. They split Germany into two regions.

2. They themselves took over Europe.

Stay tuned for further announcements.

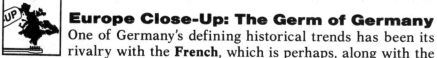

Europe Close-Up: The Germ of Germany

One of Germany's defining historical trends has been its rivalry with the **French**, which is perhaps, along with the English-French, Italian-French, Flemish-French, and Spanish-French rivalries, the most bitter in Europe. The relationship is powered by a recurring pattern in which the French **taunt** and **provoke** the Germans until they get so mad they **invade**. It started over a hundred years ago:

French (1870): We are the *bestest,* most *beautiful,* and most *cultured* people in the world! Ribbit! [The Germans attack, beating the French army in two months.]

---

[4]Woo, woo!

French (1914): We're still better than you, you slurring, square-faced polka lovers. Plus we're much prettier, we eat real cuisine instead of your leftover pig parts, and we have a coastline along the Mediterranean. . . . How's the weather up there? [The Germans attack, occupying a third of France for years.]

French (1940): We're still better than you. Did we mention our high sense of fashion, you overweight, kraut-eating lederhosen wearers? How about our wine countr—Oops, that's right, you drink only *beer.* Sniff! How provincial. Well, work hard. We're off to the art museum, and then perhaps the café for some espresso. Keep on building things for us, will you? [Germans attack, conquering the nation in less than a month.]

French (Today): Sniff. We're still better than you.

Basically, the Germans hate the French because the French've always said they're superior without ever having invented anything more clever than *chicken cordon bleu* to prove it, and the French hate the Germans for invading their country in **1917** with ground troops, in **1942** with tanks and planes, and **every summer since then** with RVs, trailers, and pooping children on their way to the Mediterranean.

Culture

This little hang-up about conquering the world hasn't done much for Germany's culture. You can tell a lot about what's important to a nation by what its city names bring to mind. Gourmet **France** has Dijon and Champagne. Flamboyant **Italy** boasts Florentine scarves and Roman holidays. Butt-cold **England** has Oxford sweaters and Cambridge wool.

So what does **Germany** have? Hamburg and Frankfurt.

Germany might not have any culture at all, were it not for **yeast cultures**.

Lamb, Lamb, Lamb: Fun with Germans

Those nutty Germans are suckers for a good authority figure. As one cab driver put it, "Why is there so little crime in Germany? Because it's against the law!" Mix this fact in with a little history, and you too can have fun with Germans!

• Wait until a traffic signal says DON'T WALK, and then start walking *back and forth, back and forth* across the road. Stop when the light says WALK, no matter where you are. Germans *hate* that.

• Nail a piece of trash to the sidewalk, sit back, and enjoy.

• Start a line! Get a few friends, and stand behind each other at a bus stop, movie theater, or department store. Watch the Germans queue up without even knowing what for!

• When speaking with Germans, casually say "Normandy" whenever you mean "normally," but act natural.

 ## Understanding Those Peculiar Natives

Germans, when not drunk, have an attitude sociologists have identified as **Classical Neo-Archie Bunkeresque**. Their strong rating on the Grump Index can be traced to two outside causes:

1. Their **weather**.[5]

2. Their **language**, which has all the charm and subtlety of a garbage disposal (You'd avoid conversation too if it involved constantly sounding like you were about to hock up *ein Big One*).

Europe Close-Up: The German Language

Most people's knowledge of German can be summed up in two words: **kindergarten** and **Schwarzkopf**.[6] The rest, they will tell you, is pretty much just English with a slur. But those poor souls are missing out on many of **German's subtle nuances:**

1. The language is **butt ugly**. Proper German has that "chainsaw cutting through a backed-up septic tank" sound to it, much like Nirvana without the long hair.

2. Germans have this habit of throwing all their verbs to the end of the sentence so that even if you're speaking it right, you still come out sounding like an overdubbed **Yoda with a saliva problem**.

3. We don't have some of their characters, like the *umlaut*. And they don't have some of ours, like *spaces in between words*.

---

[5]It's raining.
[6]translation: General Blackhead

4. Like many European languages, German has **formal** (*Sie*) and **informal** (*du*) versions of "you." These were designed by Europeans primarily as a clever way to **confuse American seventh-grade language students** and thus keep the U.S. educational system lagging far behind their own.

There are no hard-and-fast rules for when one should use either version. But in general, follow *Don't Go*'s handy rule of thumb for the German second person and/or dating in the nineties:

> You should *Sie* someone at
> least a few times before trying to *du* them.

Real Testimony: Germanic-Depressives

I wanted to know at least one language before going to Europe. Y'know, besides English. So a month or two before I made the **big mistake**,[7] I swore I'd learn as much German as possible in the little time I had. I wanted to speak German, breathe German, eat German. . . . That is, until I got a look at what eating German actually entailed.

By the time I left, I was set. I knew *four different German phrases* for asking someone to speak in English, and—as an added bonus—I also had the phrase **"Where is McDonald's?"** down pretty well.

Of course, it was all useless as soon as I got to Germany. I was resting on a bench when some **weirdo guy in black** came up to me, pointed at my water bottle, and said—this is exactly what six months of language class allowed me to hear—"Schochen schafen lafen gedoibiedoibie ja ja ja."

He then stretched out his arms and moved them in some mutant **Steve Martin** impression, waiting for me to laugh at his comment, which was apparently hilarious. I was tempted to pull the ol' **"I've no idea what you're saying so I'm just going to laugh and hope you go away" trick**, but could I just point at my ear and shake my head, the internationally recognized sign for "I am a clueless twerp"? No! I had to ask him to repeat himself. And I had to ask him *in German*.

"Um, ah . . . bitte, Sie, uh, no. Wait. Um, Können ah, sauerkraut, um . . ." C'mon, Chris! You can do it! Eye of the tiger! For the next

---

[7]my trip to Europe

ten minutes I tried to make him understand my request, sputtering, stuttering, slurring, shouting, stomping, and waving my arms in 17 different directions, as if by emphasizing my "um"s with **pterodactyl imitations** I was making the task that much easier for him.

The man just stared, obviously regretting ever having said a word to me in the first place. Every time my gestures got a little more desperate, he took a small, deliberate step backwards. I tried every single German phrase that came to mind, but the only positive response I ever got was when he pointed two blocks down the street to the nearest McDonald's.

Finally, I just pointed at my ear and shook my head. The poor man, realizing that I'd never understood him at all, walked away, dejected. He caught the subway back to his one-room apartment, fixed himself a strong cocktail, and pondered the meaning of his measly, lonely existence. What does it all mean? he asked himself. What am I living for, when even the tiniest bright moments that I have are destroyed within minutes? God, I remember the days when I made people laugh, really laugh, and life was good. But now. . . . He sighed, stirred his drink slowly, and looked out of the dirty window of his apartment onto the street below. "Yes, Anna was truly right," he muttered. When he awoke, the dinosaur was still there.

NOT *EAST* BERLIN . . . NOT *WEST* BERLIN . . . BUT BERLIN!

Berlin. One Moody City. Land of Lennon glasses and home of the most infamous **wall** in modern history besides Fenway Park's **Green Monster**. How did this all begin? Let's go back, back, back. . . .

History

After the war, Us and Them[8] split Berlin and Germany into east and west sides, the east being dirty and run-down, the west being cute and rich, modeled after the system used in **Los Angeles**. But thanks to the modern miracle of poor urban planning, *our* West Berlin was deep in *their* East Germany. *Nutty!* In 1948, the Soviets blocked off all our routes to West Berlin—trying, we guess, to starve the West Berliners into believing that they'd be better off with them.

---

[8]full name: Them Commies

Thus began the famous **Berlin Airlift**, in which essentials for daily city life were flown from the West into Berlin day after day. The Soviets finally realized, "If this keeps up, then the crappy American airplanes of the later 20th century will eventually start **dropping their engines** on our innocent East German citizens en route. We can't let that happen!" Thanks to **American engine? Ew!-ity**, we got to keep West Berlin.

It would not be until **the autumn of 1989** that Berlin was again a hot topic, and no one would ever again doubt the historical importance of Berlin. But we all know the reason for this.[9]

Europe Close-Up: The Berlin Wall

Seeing something like **the Berlin Wall** now reduced to nothing more than mantelpiece art can bring a variety of reactions. Some break down in tears. Some swell with pride. Some pee on it. For us here at *Don't Go*, however, it inspired one awe-filled response above all others, the true sign of importance in the American's mind,

"Dude, I gotta get a piece."

But the wall's sections are either gone or certified art now, and you can't just walk up and throw a sledgehammer at it now any more than you would knock a souvenir **big toe** off the **statue of David** in Florence, which we wouldn't dare recommend, since there's only one left and anyway it would be much easier to snag any of his five **fingers**.

Luckily, as you get off at **Alexanderplatz**, the East Side's main square, about 30,000 **unshaven vendors** are all waiting to help you. You may wonder where all these genuine wall pieces keep coming from. You may wonder how all the authentic spray paint got on *every side* of the chunks. You may also wonder why so many of Berlin's **sidewalks** need replacing. But what do we know?

Sights

The Checkpoint Charlie Museum: Shows all the ways that East Germans escaped into West Berlin. Our favorite was the guy who did the ol' "Hey! Es ist der Goodyear Blimp!" trick.

---

[9]It got mentioned in Billy Joel's "We Didn't Start the Fire."

The Grünewald: Berlin's main forest, it was replanted by the Germans after World War II, and is thus a forest where the trees actually grow—no kidding—*in rows.*

The Brandenburg Gate: The main gateway between East and West Sides, now a favorite hangout for shifty, concrete-hawking vendors and gullible tourists and the site of **Big Bob's World-Famous Brandenburgers**. It was here that our adventures took a tour for the worse.

 ## Europe Close-Up: European Tours
The thought of group information sessions truly brings tours to our eyes. They fall into four main categories:

The horse-and-carriage tour: These give riders a realistic idea of what authentic natives look like when they're scowling at rich foreigners parading around their city.

The city bus tour: On one of these, you can sample the highlights of the city's traffic congestion, getting a terrific view of the entrances to some of Europe's most famous attractions. You will usually listen to a prerecorded history of these entrances on bus headphones that are precisely calibrated to always remain exactly ten minutes ahead of wherever your bus happens to be at the time. If you get bored, you can switch the channels and hear what static sounds like in other languages.

The whirlwind 60-cities-in-14-days "Best of Europe's Greatest Hits" Churchathon bus tour: People who choose to join these tours are in effect joining the Cult of Polyester Casual Wear. Surrounded by other "Growing Pains"–loving Americans, they get almost no contact with locals, no intimate understanding of the various cultures, and no more than a superficial glimpse of Europe's most clichéd sites. We highly recommend it.

The walking tour: These are given by a state-certified Nerd, and the highlight is passing by an object which is the **somethingest something in all of Europe**—usually either the largest town square or the oldest Jewish temple (there are about 30 of each throughout Europe).

Accommodations

Youth hostile: Roving angry young skinheads bearing chains and lead pipes will be more than happy to put you out for the night. Minorities welcome.

Long-term housing: Fergetit. Looking for apartments in Berlin is like looking for the nonsmoking section in Spain. Ever since the wall fell and thousands have entered the city, people have clung even tighter to what housing they've got, once again proving that even after reunification, some boarders are more difficult to remove than ever.

Entertainment

Kreuzberg is the "alternative"[10] section of Berlin. Everything here in Kreuzberg is **black**: the lighting, the clothes, the layer of soot, the market. . . . Everything, that is, but the **people**. This is **young bald Easterner** territory, and they don't like folks that aren't their type—you know: "Hey! There's someone who isn't a **pasty, ugly kid** with **bad skin**! Let's get him!" Skinheads make up for their high alcohol tolerance by failing miserably in other areas. If nothing else, they prove the oft-suspected theory, "the shorter the hair, the more conservative the head."

The favorite pastime of the Kreuzberg turtlenecked, espresso-depresso, Nietzsche-keen crowd is **going out dancing alone** with mean, "I could care less about humanity" looks on their faces, engaging in the jolly pursuit of trying to convince each other that they are having the absolute *worst* time and would *much* rather be doing *anything* else, such as passing a kidney stone. Any hint of enjoyment is grounds for getting kicked out of most Berlin clubs; we recommend that while dancing you occasionally announce out loud

"Ja, I am having a most miserable time hier!"

One laugh and you'll be out on the street, subjected to bitter taunts

---

[10]weird

like, "Happiness—pfft! How shallow," accompanied by ugly stares. *Really* ugly.

Europe Close-Up: Those Ugly Germans

OK, we're Americans, and we're Ugly. We accept it. Gee whiz, you could fill a scrapbook with pictures of all the European sculptures I've peed on during my travels. No wonder Europeans aren't surprised when various statistics appear showing that the average American thinks Albania is the capital of New York, considers it possible that the 1800s never really occurred, and couldn't beat an answering machine in chess.

But Germans ooze a more external, facial-hair-related kind of ugliness. It's not just that they're, um, *big-boned*. Hm, how shall we explain this? Does *attractively challenged* mean anything to you?

People in America have **bad hair days**. People in Germany have **bad face days**. Often.

Over the years, they've developed different ways of coping:

Frankfurt: Work like a slave! The problems of ugliness in one's social life thus never surface, because one *has* no social life.

Munich: Ingest large quantities of German beer! Suddenly, no one's all that ugly anymore! Or is that a lamppost?

Berlin: Cover it up! For this glorious cause, Berliners put on Cher clothing, Elvira makeup, and Chernobyl hair dye. They wear their earrings in strange ways, like in their eyebrows. They put on nose-rings, nipplerings, inh-your-tongue-tho-you-talk-wike-thith-rings. Thus they avoid the "ugly" label by dressing to look as downright hideous as possible.

NOT *EAST* BONN . . . NOT *WEST* BONN . . . BUT—AAAHH, SCREW IT

If it's in Germany, why is it called **Bonn**, like the French word? Shouldn't it be called **Gutt**? And shouldn't the French city **Nice** be **Joli** instead? And then there's **Reykjavík**. . . .

BAVARIA

Ah, Bavaria, where the one-two one-two polka beat never goes out of style, where the more hip you have, the more hip you are, and the only place in the world where balding, pot-bellied, weeble wobble–shaped men can get away with wearing **leather pants**. Ah, Bavaria! Ah, humanity! It must bavarian-usual, this place, but we're here to tell y'all about it so *you* don't have to go.

Munich

Munich, The City of Sticky Sidewalks, has two kinds of attractions: the kind you pound, and the kind you'll lie in bed not seeing because you pounded too much of the first attraction the night before.

History

Munich has a fascistnating past, and its residents would just as soon you forget all about it.

Sights

C'mon, forget that **clock with the things that move on it**. Forget the **naked flower people** singing about peace, love, and other outdated topics in the **Englischer Garten**, a.k.a. Bare-assic Park. Sure, they're *really nude*, but frankly the thought of **naked Germans** is the kind of thing that keeps us up at night in a cold sweat. And forget the **churches**. For God's sake, get a grip and forget the churches.

But whatever you do, don't forget your Tums and Tylenol.

Food

Planning to eat in Germany? Two words to live by: **Top Ramen**.

German food is unique in the world for combining both **lousy taste** and an incredible **lack of nutritional value**. Even *Let's Go* calls it "generally fatty and ponderous." Translation: After a few days of eating greasy, fatty German food, your face will break out into one gigantic, throbbing **pimple**.

The four German food groups are **beer, sauerkraut, another beer**, and the most perfectly named substance ever besides maybe flubber, **wurst**. There must be about 700 kinds of wurst: *Blutwurst*,[11] *Grosswurst, EvenGrosserwurst, Zis-Schtuff-Is-So-Gross-*

---

[11]That's blood sausage, by the way.

Ve-Vouldn't-Feed-It-to-Ein-Schtarving-Dogwurst. Munich is Germany's number one "too-wurst attraction."

DON'T GO'S CONCISE HISTORY IN DRAMATIC FORM OF THE CREATION OF THE WURST

[The curtain opens on a butcher's shop in the Middle Ages. Two piles—one of **hollow pig intestines**, the other of random **leftover pig parts**—lie in a bloody mess on the floor. Enter Butcher, who looks at one pile, then the other, then the first pile, then the second again.]

Butcher: Hey, I've got a funny idea! . . .

The End

 While in Munich, you'd better stick to safe American food like hot dogs.

Entertainment

But let's face it. If you're in Munich, and we dare say Don't Go, then you have just one cultural activity on your mind: to **drink yourself silly** while some **oom-pah band** plays "Beer Barrel Polka" in the background.

Munich's most famous drinking establishment is the **Hofbräuhaus**, which is a cross between a beer hall, a bad frat party, and Mall of America.

The Hofbräuhaus is big, and we mean real big—Schwarzenegger big—deficit big—Africa big—that-ball-of-twine-in-Kansas big. Big BIG **BIG**! It also should have a large, flashing neon sign outside it that warns

LARGEST COLLECTION OF
AMERICAN COLLEGE STUDENTS
EAST OF DAYTONA BEACH
—SINCE 1979—

Oktoberfest, Novemberfest, breakfast . . . All year round, thousands of Ugly Americans are in this establishment for the sole and lofty purpose of getting **skunked off their rears**. Rows of large wooden tables stretch back over the horizon, each crowded with young Americans swinging mugs the size of Japanese automobiles against each other and gaily pouring beer on their heads. A traditional oom-pah band plays the traditional **"Beer Barrel Polka"** over and over (and *over* and *over*), while the just-as-traditional **blue-faced-lightweights-racing-to-the-toilets-in-back parade** charms spectators nightly. Don't stand in the front row.

 ## Europe Close-Up: The Hofbräuhaus Experience

The typical night at the Hofbräuhaus goes something like this:

Sit down! Waiter brings a round of beers and some pretzels and makes a quick toast. "Prost!" everyone shouts, and takes a big gulp.

"Beer Barrel Polka" starts playing. Everyone laughs.

Next round! Waiter brings a bunch of beers and makes a quick toast. "Prooost!" everyone shouts, and takes a messy gulp.

"Beer Barrel Polka" starts playing. Everyone laughs and swings their steins along to the beat.

Next round! Waiter swings by, drops off some pretzels and another round of beers, and makes a big toast. "Prooashh!" everyone shouts, and pours beer down their shirts.

"Beer Barrel Polka" starts playing. Everyone laughs and gets up and dances, instantly bonding with a random group of equally drunk cuties from Michigan.

Next round! Waiter runs by, replaces basket of pretzels, drops off a bunch of beers, and makes a huge toast. "Raaaghhh!" everyone shouts, and throws beer onto their faces.

"Beer Barrel Polka" starts playing. A few get up to dance until the Michigan cuties say they're gonna puke if they have to hear that damn song one more time. Everyone quickly agrees and collapses back on the bench.

Next round! Waiter throws down some more beers and makes a hearty toast. "Uuuuungh!" everyone moans as they take a cautious sip, cover their mouths, and race blue-faced to the toilets in back.

"Beer Barrel Polka" starts playing. Michigan cuties make good on their promise.

On the ground! Wake up lying in a urine-soaked alleyway, still in yesterday's clothes, smelling of puke-breath, with your camera, travelers' checks, and underwear missing, a military jet show performing against your temples, and vague recollections of making out with something which resembled a golden retriever floating through one's aching head.

Accommodations

Jugendhergerge Youth Hostel, Wendl-Dietrich-Str. At this gray, dirty, and crowded hostel, you'll find 38 people in line for each arctic-water shower in the morning and be served stale bread, hard cheese, and suspiciously yellow tea for breakfast. It's your average youth hostel.

Urine-Soaked Alleyway. Conveniently located next to the Hofbräuhaus, this is a favorite spot for lone travelers who've drunk so much that they'd sleep on gravel[12] if that's all there was. The cost is steep—you'll wake up without your passport, camera, and travelers' checks. An additional downside is the possibility of being arrested by the Munich police. Now, in case your knowledge of history is a bit average, let's just say that you do *not* want to mess with the Munich police. But you can't beat the location.

Near Munich

Putting the "Ich!" back into Munich are a few lovely **tourist repulsions**. First is the site of the **1972 Summer Olympics**, whose mascot, you may recall, was a cute little furry animal holding an AK-47. If that's not enough for you, then swing by **Dachau**, "My Very First Concentration Camp" for Germany and **Official Birthplace of the Most Loathesome Period in Human History Which Is Actually Saying Quite a Lot**. Of course, 22 percent of Americans believe it's possible that the Holocaust didn't occur at all. Coincidentally, this is the same percentage of people who watch "Larry King Live" on a regular basis.

But the most depressingest site of all is the **BMW Museum**, where the tour guide will be more than happy to point out that you

---

[12]or even on an airplane flight

will never in your entire puny, excremental existence on Earth earn enough to purchase *any* of the vehicles you see here displayed.

Europe Close-Up: Otto's Autos

There are three main types of German car. The snottiest is the **BMW**, short for "**bite my weenie**," which is what most people who drive them are telling the rest of the world. Unfortunately for them, the rest of us take BMW to mean "**break my windshield.**"

Trading in quality for quantity is the **Volkswagen**. Volkswagen's driving principle is the word *Fahrvergnügen*, as in, "AAAAH!!! These *fahrvergnügen* brakes don't work!" The word is derived from the Latin phrase *Ius fahrfignutinus trustus sic es throlus*, which means "I trust this fig newton about as far as I can throw it."

Finally, **East Germany**'s best, worst, and only car was the **Trabante**, a German word meaning "Edsel." On the evolutionary scale of cars, the "Trabi," as it would have been affectionately called had anyone ever held affection for it, is slightly higher than a **tin can** and slightly lower than the **Flintstones' car**.

The Trabante was *the* East German car. That's all there was, unless you were a high-ranking government official. You can imagine what it was like trying to find your car in a **mall parking lot**. "Thank God we live in Eastern Europe!" people would often say. "Otherwise, we might actually have a reason to go to our malls and then we'd *never* be able to find our car!"

FUSSEN

Füssen's most famous sight is the **Euro Disney Castle** which, due to a minor surveying error, was erected approximately 433 miles from the rest of the park. You may have seen pictures of this castle standing majestically on a hill against a clear blue background— friendly, inviting.

Lies, lies, *lies!* Every time we tried to visit this town, it started raining Katzen und Hunde, as they often say there, and the temperature dropped faster than a male Kennedy's boxer shorts.

That's all that we can tell you about Füssen, because we here at *Don't Go* had eaten a big Mexican meal in Munich the night before visiting it.

Don't Go's Fundamental Rule of Traveling: Never, never, ever eat Mexican food in Europe. Although one of us had already cleared out his system in a Hofbräuhaus sink, the rest of us still felt like we might at any moment hit the reverse button on the great tape player of food digestion, and besides, there's no use in Füssen anyway, so we laid low.

HEIDELBERG

Heidelberg is a small college town near Frankfurt. Thank you.

Food

For a quick bite, don't miss **Big Bob's World-Famous Heidelburgers**.

Sights

Heidelberg's big tourist draw is **Heidelberg Castle**, an exquisite, moss-ridden **pile of bricks** that you must climb approximately 20,000,000,000,000,000 stairs up a hill to see. If you actually make it up, you will probably want to celebrate by partaking in the ancient tourist tradition of **puking over the edge of the castle**. Heads up while climbing.

Avoid at All Costs

Also on top, you will be rewarded with the once-in-a-lifetime chance to see the **world's largest barrel**, housed inside the castle. They charge almost a buck for this sight, making most of their money off **dumb Americans** who, when confronted with the opportunity, are afraid that they will hate themselves forever if they travel all the way to Heidelberg and pass up on the chance to see something as amazingly remarkable as the world's largest barrel.

But you're smarter than that. We can tell, you bought our book. So we have only two words for you: Don't Go! Don't be fooled! Do you really want to know what the world's largest barrel looks like? Just follow our simple instructions here, and we'll **save you bucks**:

Step 1: Picture an average, ordinary, run-of-the-mill barrel—the kind you run into every day on the streets.

Step 2: Now, picture this same exact barrel, except really, really, really, really, really, really, really, really, really big.

FRANKFURT

Frankfurt is a large, unfriendly financial center filled with dirty, gray office high-rises, thus earning it the title **the Most American-ized City in Europe**.

Sights
There are no sights in Frankfurt.

Accommodations
Screw accommodations. Get out while you can. Hitchhike if you must.

Europe Close-Up: Hitchhiking in Europe
In the United States, **hitchhiking** is a fairly simple process. You just find a nice **highway**, stick out your **thumb**, get into the first **car** that stops, and wind up mangled and battered in a backwoods **ditch** three states over. Simple.

In America, if you hitchhike, you're either crazy or stupid. If you pick up hitchhikers, you're either crazy or stupid. If either person involved is crazy, the ride gets violently aborted at the first deserted stretch of highway. So the only time hitchhiking in America actually might work is when two stupid people ride with each other, in which case they'll probably get lost or forget where they were going anyway.

In America, hitchhiking is most successful in the Midwest. Go figure. But in Europe, hitchhiking is a whole ritual. First of all, you gotta look good. Try on that new suit! Break out the mink wrap! No one's gonna pick you up if you look crazy—unless, of course, there's a really lost Midwesterner tooling around your area.

Secondly, the hand signals are more complex. Again, in America, it's an easy system: Hold up your **thumb** as a car approaches, and your **middle finger** as it drives by. But in Poland, for example, you stick out your entire hand like you're trying to give the car a high five.[13] In Romania, you wave a pack of Marlboros. In Yugoslavia, you shoot the windshield.

But in subdued, efficient **Germany**, you just hold out a cute little piece of cardboard with the initial of the city you want to get to. How quaint.

Real Testimony: Life's a Hitch

I stood near a highway entrance ramp in romantic Frankfurt. It was just past noon, and I needed to get across the country to Berlin in time to sleep through class early the next morning. I had 14 hours, no money, and the side of an old cardboard box I'd picked out of a dumpster. I had the **itch to hitch**, honey.

Now, I knew hitching in Europe was a delicate operation. And when it comes to delicate operations, I'm all thumbs. So I thought I'd be a phenomenal hitchhiker.

But my big mistake was the cardboard sign. Instead of just writing a black *B* for Berlin like any other motor-moocher would, I tried to compose a minor German novel on my piece of cardboard:

BERLIN OR AS FAR AS POSSIBLE

Poetic, eh? I spent half an hour on that sign, carefully measuring out the spaces between letters, filling in penciled outlines with calligraphic flourishes . . . but in the end, thanks to my somewhat rusty German skills, I mixed up a couple words and ended up writing what translates to:

"Berlin or how far so possible"

It means as little in their language as it does in ours. But I was clueless. Me and my stupid sign walked down to the highway entrance and started our work.

---

[13]One encounters a disproportionate number of hitchhikers with broken arms in Poland.

This was it. I was really hitchhiking, completely violating everything my mother had ever told me about strange cars and free candy. I hadn't felt this rebellious since I'd danced to Twisted Sister's "We're Not Gonna Take It" back in ninth grade. I was on the road with a backpack, just like Bill Bixby at the end of an "Incredible Hulk" show, except no one was whistling that silly little tune in my ear.

I stood out there for two hours, holding up my stupid sign for every passing supremist German to laugh at. They all twisted up their faces as they went. I scoffed, assuming it was because they couldn't believe the sight of such a rebellious, Dylanesque dude as me actually hitchhiking on their autobahn; really it was because they couldn't figure out what the hell my sign said.

They probably thought I was from the Midwest.

I waited a while longer without luck, realized I'd been waving my sign at traffic going in the wrong direction, crossed the road, and almost immediately, a beat-up van pulled over. I ran up, but before I even got in, the fifty-year-old woman driving snapped at me in German, "You shouldn't hitchhike. It's dangerous." *Thanks, Mom.* I almost replied, "Well, you shouldn't pick up hitchhikers. It's just as dangerous." But that strategy struck me as pretty stupid, since there was always the chance she'd agree with me and tell me to get out. Besides, you just don't mess with German mother figures.

We spoke for a while in English, then she asked me what I was doing in Germany. When I told her I was a student, she let out a loud "Ach! Wir müssen Deutsch sprechen!" ("Ack! We must German speak! Then Jedi will you be!") and from then on, refused to speak or listen to a single word of English. I tried in vain to explain that my knowledge of German was limited to simple verbs, classroom objects, and asking where the nearest McDonald's was, but she refused to listen.

For a while, I tried to rise to the occasion, attempting to spark heated debates on such subjects as metric rulers and double cheeseburgers. But in every sentence I spoke, there would always be a word I didn't know. So I'd try to explain, in German, the definition of the word I didn't know, except that in my definition, there was another word I didn't know that I needed to know. So I'd give *another* explanation. . . . Pretty soon I learned to shut up and just nod my head whenever she spoke.

She told me she was going through some podunk town in Eastern Germany and handed me a map of Austria so I could locate it. This clever little brain teaser kept me occupied for a good twenty minutes.

Then we started to chat. Or, she started to chat. I pretended to listen.

After a month's immersion in this language, I had developed a system of which I was fairly proud:

HOW TO HOLD A CONVERSATION IN A FOREIGN LANGUAGE WITHOUT UNDERSTANDING A SINGLE FLIPPIN' WORD THE OTHER PERSON IS SAYING

For each sentence spoken ask the speaker to repeat herself.
Assuming you still don't understand,
then listen to her tone of voice.

IF IT SOUNDS LIKE	THEN SAY
A fact	"Hm, that's interesting"
An opinion	"Yes, I believe that also"
A joke	"Ha ha ha. Very funny."
They're pointing something out	"Yes, I see. Very beautiful"
A command	"*You* do it"
You have no idea what it sounds like	"Yes, I understand"

This method should have been a raging success, but most of the time, people were asking me **questions**. A typical moment during the ride:

Helga: Damn, there's traffic up ahead.
Me: Excuse me?
Helga: Traffic jam in front of us.
Me: Ah, yes, I see. Very beautiful.

Helga:	So, where in the States are you from?
Me:	Excuse me?
Helga:	Where are you from?
Me:	Hm, that's interesting.
Helga:	Where?
Me:	Oh . . . Berlin. But just take me how far so possible.
Helga:	No, where in the United States do you come from?
Me:	Ha ha ha. Very funny.
Helga:	What?
Me:	Yes, I understand. [There's a half-minute pause until I finally realize she was asking me something.] Oh, excuse me. Connecticut.
Helga:	Ah, the East Coast! You seem more like a Midwesterner.
Me:	Yes, I believe that also.

Fortunately, she didn't understand my German any more than I understood hers, so I was saved from complete embarrassment.

Two hours later, I was back in Berlin. Just before going to bed, I took one last look at my sign, noticed the two-foot-long grammatical error that I'd been waving at cars all day, and decided to move to Indiana.

We close our chapter on **those nutty Germans** with a small disclaimer: Sure, we've been harsh in this chapter, but one should know that it's only unfair to make fun of disadvantaged or underprivileged groups.[14] Germans, on the other hand, *are* the **Master Race**, thus they're fair game.

---

[14]unless it's the **French**; then go right ahead

Boots went out of fashion years ago; Italy is now shaped like a cross-trainer.

Let's Eat
Italy

The government's asunder
From corruption here in Italy.
It makes you think "No wonder
Everything here runs so—er, poorly."

ITALY
VITAL INFORMATION

Currency in use: The libra

Dominant stereotype: Name-calling, bocce-balling, opera-singing, pasta-flinging, unshaven, sexist, chest-beating family men

Official motto: Inscribed on all old buildings: SENATVS POPVLVSQVE ROM—VH, GVYS? WHAT'S VP WITH OVR U'S? THEY'RE ALL TVRNING OVT JVST LIKE V'S!

Theme song: "Sicily Love Songs"

For fun: Bocce ball!

Contributions to American culture: *Rocky I–V, The Godfather I–III, Super Mario Brothers I–II*

Ugly American visits, returns with: Twelve souvenir shoes, twelve souvenir scarves, twelve souvenir pounds

Overall rating (−10 to 0): −5

How to sound like you've really, truly been there: Vowels, m'boy, vowels at the ends of your words. They'll never know the difference.

Italy is a long country, with a long history, long noodles, and even longer lunch breaks. It is also the only place in Europe where you will stand out as a tourist if you do *not* communicate by waving your hands around wildly.

If you visit Italy, which you shouldn't, then keep in mind the phrase "When in Rome, do as the Romans do." That is, do nothing.

Understanding Those Peculiar Natives
The most important and only uncorrupted institution in Italy is the **family**, headed by **Mama**. Mama leads the daily ritual of **dinner**, for which the typical family—spanning more

generations than the Old Testament—gathers every night into a kitchen about the size of a Playmate cooler to cook **pasta**, since it's an easy dish for large crowds. Here they cook and cook and TALK REALLY LOUDLY AT THE SAME TIME AS EVERYONE ELSE and eat and eat and eat until the newlyweds start fighting and the man tries to shake her violently into believing he respects her, to which she responds with a salvo of dirty lasagna dishes until one hits him in the eye and they both feel awful and apologize and reunite and retire to the back room to make violent, passionate love. Meanwhile, the rest of the family reemerges from under the sink and goes out for **gelato**, which everyone knows is just French for ice cream.

There's another kind of family in Italy, almost as violent, but we'll get to that later.

History
Over the course of Europe's round-robin wars, Italians have crafted an unparalleled reputation for **dropping their pants and running**. After two world wars, one standard joke involved a classified ad: FOR SALE: 30,000 ITALIAN GUNS. NEVER BEEN FIRED; DROPPED TWICE.

During World War II Italy told its ally, Germany, "OK, you take care of the United States and all of Europe, and, uh, we'll make sure **Ethiopia** doesn't give us any trouble." We're certain there was *quite* a bit of civic pride over ransacking an underdeveloped desert nation. Funny thing is, they still ended up getting their Axis kicked.

Italian war heroes? You'd be better off looking for German health food or English slapstick.

Europe Close-Up: Italian Men
The Italian man is in a class—and possibly species—all by himself. But once you get through his big talk, big ego, and big chest hair, you'll find a sweet, lovable—Wait! Where'd he go?

Aha, just kidding! Really! C'mon Vinny, I was just—ow! Stop it!

The first thing you must realize is that you should **never pick on Italian men**. They're very sensitive to ridicule and tend to deal with it in ways that involve brass knuckles and concrete mix. And they'll fight you over anything, even, tee hee, soccer, because Italians know that trying to solve every problem with fists is a sign of **masculinity**. In that case Italians are *incredibly* masculine, masculine being a synonym for *immature*, and they love to strut around half-naked, chests hyperinflated, with their arms sticking out in some Christ-like pose so everyone can smell just how masculine they are. Grunting and chest-beating and butting heads during the mating season are all common rituals for Italian men. It's enough to make you think they *invented* the word **machismo**.

But *fawwwwk!* This is only one dimension of the Italian man, and Italian men are almost always at least two-dimensional. Their quickness to anger is just one example of their overall **passion** for life. They eat passionately, love passionately, eat some more passionately, take a very passionate nap, wake up and have a cold, passionate pasta sandwich, and then trudge off to work, where they passionately do as little as possible in the short time they are there.

In America, this passion has meant big bucks on the big screen, as Italian-American men have captured the hearts of millions, often against the millions' will. What woman is there who would not swoon over the mere mention of such hunks-a hunks-a burnin' love as **Joe Pigato**, **Danny DeVito**, and the original Zip-Loc man himself, **Dom DeLuise**?

But there is a problem with male Italian/Italian-American entertainers. They seem to be getting larger and larger:

FAMOUS ITALIAN ENTERTAINER	STARTED OUT	ENDED UP
Marlon Brando	Skinny	Fat
Frank Sinatra	Skinny	Fat
Luciano Pavarotti/ Dom DeLuise*	Fat	Fatter
John Belushi	Fat	Fat and Dead
Tony Curtis	Skinny	Fat
Tony Danza	Skinny	Not much fatter but the lead in "Who's the Boss?" which we consider a fate worse than fat

Robert DeNiro and **Al Pacino** beware: *Raging Bologna* and *Scarf Ace* could be coming soon to a (wide-screen) theater near you.

---

*We could never tell the two apart anyway.

Lamb, Lamb, Lamb: Mangia, Mangia, Mangia!

They say you can tell a lot about what's important in a culture by what things they have many names for. Eskimos, for example, have over a hundred names for snow. Los Angelosers have a similar number for smog. Italians, it seems, have given a different name to **each individual piece of pasta** ever created, names like *Lamborghini* and *Spicoli* and *Mini Ravioli with Meatballs*. There were at press time over 41,874,986,300,000,000 types of pasta, approximately 41,874,986,300,000,000 of which taste exactly like all the others.

This can be confusing, especially since so many famous Italians have names that could be pasta dishes. In our opinion, there's nothing more embarrassing than sitting down in an Italian restaurant, ordering a plate of **hot Mancini**, and a half hour later having the waiter throw a CD on your table with Tower Records security right on his tail. To help you avoid these jams, we've included the following reference chart:

Is It a Person or a Pasta Dish?		
NAME	**PERSON**	**PASTA DISH**
Manicotti		✔
Righetti	✔	
Mussolini	✔	
Fettuccine		✔
Al Fredo		✔
Al Pacino	✔	
Fonzarelli	✔	
Cannelloni		✔
Buttafuoco	✔	

> And remember, **gelato** is the French word for ice cream; **Gerardo** was the flash-in-the-pan lambada-pop singer. Never, ever ask for Gerardo for dessert, and whatever you do, don't put gelato in your cassette player.

 ## Transportation

If you rely on the train system in Italy, allow for a little extra time to get to your destination,[1] for the train union will probably be on **strike**. Italian unions and workers strike at least four or five times a year, more if the weather holds up. This is not political; it is simply their collective version of the sick day.

> ***Worker 1:*** I don't feel like working today.
> ***Worker 2:*** Neither do I.
> ***Worker 1:*** Let's strike!
> ***Worker 2:*** OK!

This is just one striking example of Italy's economic structure, in which people can wait over a month just to get a phone line installed, known as **lazy-faire economics**.

VENICE

Congratulations! You've just turned to Venice, the only city in the world whose major attraction is a **flooded sewer system**! It flows! It leaks! It reeks! "Venice the next train out of here?" we ask.

Motorist alert: All the roads are flooded in Venice. People either putt around in little *On-Golden-Pond*esque motorboats or pole their way on **gondolas** through the sludge, rotten fruit cores, and crumpled wads of toilet paper.

---

[1]Three to four weeks is usually sufficient.

There are some other hassles.

TOP FIVE ROAD PROBLEMS UNIQUE TO VENICE

5. Electric bus lines keep killing all their passengers.

4. Little old lady in huge paddleboat hogging up entire lane.

3. In small collisions, have to get out of vehicle and yell at other driver while treading water.

2. Inner city kids turning off fire hydrants, drying up roads.

1. Have to repaint that dotted center line every few minutes.

Sights

Venice is split down the middle by the **Canal Grande**, a large-intestine-shaped passage whose water actually *looks* like what you would expect to find in someone's large intestine. If you ride a water taxi all the way down it and out through the "anus" of Venice, you will find yourself at the famous **Piazza del Pigeon Droppings**.

Tourists gather in droves to watch the legendary Winged Rats of Venice magically turn bread crumbs into little squirts of sticky white stuff before their very eyes. Be sure to pick up some souvenirs!

Entertainment

Going for a boat ride? You have our gondolences.

If you plan to ride a **gondola** in Venice, then you may want to pack some extra items, for example: a **lawyer** to help you draw up that **second mortgage**.

Nighttime gondola rides cost about **$100 an hour**, and in lire $100 translates to approximately half the paper capacity of the state of Oregon. Sane people will recognize this amount as **too much**. But sane people are generally not the type that visit Europe in the first place.

Besides, take one look at the long, romantic boat with the Bob's Big Boy curl in its front. Now take another look at **River Styx Man**—you know, the guy in pole position with baggy black knickers, a horizontal-red-and-white-striped spandex T-shirt, and that *stupid* beret that looks like a big sun-dried tomato on his head and that makes you feel like socking him right in his George Michael scruff. You'll be hooked! Just like a thousand families before you with a similar lack of concern for their financial future:

"Oh, let's ride the gondola, snookums!"

"I don't think so, pooky-love. Why don't we save some money and buy a small Caribbean island instead?"

"I wanna me ride the boat!"

"Oh, see? Junior here wants to ride it!"

"Junior here is sounding more and more like he's *from* Italy. We'd better not expose him to any more contact."

Then comes the clincher. "I CAN'T BELIEVE WE'VE COME ALL THE WAY TO VENICE, AND WE'RE NOT EVEN GOING TO RIDE A GONDOLA!"

And so, to avoid an international incident, all higher brain functions that separate humans from mollusks are shoved aside and the now-happy-but-homeless family trudges back to their apartment to secure the appropriate number of suitcases of Italian lire.

VERONA

Verona was the setting for *Romeo and Juliet*, an old-fashioned, unrequited-love *West Side Story* rip-off about the conflict between the Montagues and Capulets, best summed up in the famous lines:

Romeo: Forsooth Juliet, I'm Montague pretty badly right now!
Juliet: Nay, forget it! 'Tis no chance of thou Capuleting with me![2]

Accommodations
Some women opt to stay in **nunneries** while traveling in Italy, but frankly the thought of keeping a **10:30 P.M. curfew** in a place where the only fun you'll have is if you can figure out where they stash the extra bottles of the blood of Christ should be enough to make anyone cloisterphobic.

---

[2] *Romeo and Juliet: The Lost Episodes*, fifth quarto, first folio, act I, scene iii, lines 45–46, Member FDIC

FLORENCE

Speak of Florence, and some will imagine its romantic waterways and beautiful bridges. Others will think of the exotic art. All we think of is **Florence Henderson**, "Brady Bunch" Supermom. Many, however, will think "Eat, eat, eat!" or "Shop, shop, shop!," and the rest of us will be left thinking we're in a big, virtual reality "Cathy" comic strip.

Florence is also a favorite spot for American colleges' Have Your Parents Pay Us Wads o' Cash So You Can "Study Abroad" While You Sample the Local Alcoholic Beverages and We Won't Tell Programs. Most of these "academic villas" are just (way) off-campus frat/sorority houses; Florence study groups tend to accept more Greeks than Italians into their programs.

 ## Sights

It's **museum madness** in Florence! The most famous one is the **Uffizi Museum/Bomb Shelter**, which was hit by **terrorists** last year and has since changed its name to the **Uzi Museum**. Inside you will find works by such famous Italians as **Michelangelo**, **Donatello** and **Raphael**, a group of artists classified in America as **Ninja Turtles**.

In the nearby **Accademia** is the famous **statue of David**, and never have we seen a finer display of **Accademia nuts**. This sculpture is important historically, for it proves an oft-disputed Biblical fact: David actually slew Goliath **in the buff**. That was his trick. Goliath laughed so hard when he saw this **naked guy** walking up to him that David was able to whack him on the head without any trouble.

The city's **big ol' church** is the *duomo*. If you like you can take a few days climbing up it and then from the top have fun pointing out all the places in the city where you'd rather be.

 ## Food

Eating in a restaurant is one of the most quintessentially Italian activities one can experience, besides, of course, **being gunned down** in one.

The waiters are large, friendly folks who will graciously attempt to fill you up on the **house wine** while they graciously add a few extra zeros to the end of your bill. Tourists using **Italian lire** have more trouble with zeros than the Pacific fleet did. Italians intentionally express their currency in thousands because they know it will confuse tourists, most of whom would rather just go ahead and tip a waiter a full month's wages than deal with scientific notation.

Most Italian restaurants prefer to lure tourists in with a real cheap "fixed price" meal, and then subtly add a few extra charges on your bill:

A TYPICAL ITALIAN RESTAURANT BILL (FOR TWO)

Cover charge ["For a restaurant?"] 6,000

2 meals at 10,000 lire each ["Honey, that's cheap!"] 20,000

1 bottle of special blend house wine 10,000

8 breadsticks from the bowl on the table 8,000

6 patties of butter..3,000

2 cups special blend house coffee + cream and
sugar tray 5,000

2 glasses special blend house water + paper
umbrellas...3,000

2 after-dinner mints 1,000

⅕ of candle..500

Seat rental 4,000

2 × 2 hours' consumption special blend
house oxygen 10,000

Tax surcharge..4,500

Generous tip including service surcharge.................10,000

Processińg fee 5,000

English translation surcharge 6,000

Chump surcharge..7,000

La damaggio...**103,000**

Grazie!

Entertainment

If you'd like to spend your evening in the traditional Italian way, then go to a **disco** and try to pick up Americans.

Discos live down to their name. Every night the continent's slimiest, dirtiest citizens crawl forth from their pools of ooze and make their pilgrimage to these Euro-grease pits. Picture the Jersey coast with sideburns. Here they stand around watching out for foreigners on whom they can try out their **witty, newly learned English phrases**, like "Hello, my name is Alfonse. You are the most beautiful woman in the world. Would you care to be having with me a one night stand? No? OK." (Moves down the line.) "Hello, my name is Alfonse. You are the most beautiful woman in the world. . . ."

After paying an entrance fee which is indirectly proportional to how much the doorman would like to sleep with you, you'll enter a dark room with '70s lighting and **whiny Euro-dance-synth-schmaltz pop music** that's so bad that after a few minutes you'll be practically *begging* Alfonse to take you away.

PISA

Pisa is a small city crammed with gobs of tourists who've come from thousands of miles away to witness for themselves Pisa's amazingly remarkable sight of **faulty architecture**. Frankly, we wonder if these tourists are not lacking a **brain stem**.

ROME

Rome, if you want to. But don't say we didn't warn you. The first thing you will realize about Rome is that it is **17-dimensional**. There is no other way to explain how you can set off from, say, **the Colosseum** heading east, stumble through a few twisty alleys and piazzas, and suddenly find yourself at a sight somewhere far *west* of where you started—say, **Denver**. This actually happened to us once. It took us quite some time to find our way back, so bring a good map.

History

Rome was founded by two brothers, **Romulus** and **Remus**, who according to legend were raised by wolves, which explains why to this day Romans exhibit **atrocious table manners**.

Next came a long era in which people built lots and lots of **ruins**, which you can still see today, although some are in a state of disrepair. Romans also discovered the **arch**, an important architectural advancement without which we would not have such vital cultural objects as **McDonald's** today.

Finally, Romans are responsible for **Latin**, a language described by those who know it as beautiful, generous, and full of life—with phrases often used to describe the **dead**. From Latin we get the phrase *e pluribus unum*, a motto synonomous with the **American spirit** because it appears on all our **money**.

Caesar, Rome's first emperor, was considered a bit of a kook by his friends because he walked around with **laurel leaves** on his head (the world's first **really bad toupee**). Nonetheless he conquered France and England, the last time Italy would ever manage *that* trick.

But you could hear the horror movie soundtrack a cubit away: "BrutusBrutusBrutusBrutus . . . Killkillkillkill . . ." A bloody thing happened on the way to the Forum: Caesar was backstabbed by his rival **Brutus**,[3] and survived only long enough to utter the famous last words which sealed his immortality:

Well, we actually can't remember what they were. But we're sure they were very famous and inspiring.

But the salad days were over, and soon after Caesar came **Nero the Zero**, who had a popular party trick which he called **fiddling while Rome burns**, a clever stunt for which our modern leaders use the **saxophone**.

Perhaps, then, sax and violins *is* the main cause of civilization's downfall.

Around this time started the **circuses**, in which crowds gathered to watch **Christians getting eaten by lions**. Yawn. The empire split in two, but as they say, a house divided against itself is a duplex, and both parts soon collapsed under pressure from such

---

[3]Bluto in the old B&W versions

invaders as, in the "Whoa! I'm shaking in my sandals!" department, **French barbarians.**[4]

These conquerors destroyed many of the city's legendary structures, including the **Roman baths**, which you will notice Italians have apparently not yet bothered to repair.

Practical Information

Tipping: As in most of Europe, restaurants in Italy really go the extra kilometer for their customers by calculating their generous tip *for you* and including it right in your bill! Not satisfied with the service, though? Here's the only tip you need: Next time you want Italian, *Let's Go: Domino's!*

Laundromats: closed.

Post office: closed.

Embassies: closed.

Buses: orange.

Europe Closed-Up: Southern Standard Time

Despite what you were supposed to have learned in middle school, the sun does not give humans energy. It saps it. Look at the Germans. They have no sun and oodles of cars and ATM machines and things that make loud noises. Now, look at Italy. They have plenty of sun and long nappy-poos, and "being there sharp" means show up on the right day, please. Time is a very general concept down here. As one observer put it, "The only place Italians ever worry about seconds is at the dinner table."

Sights

Many myths have built up around this city. Our favorite is that Rome wasn't built in a day. Hey, someone's obviously never seen Rome! It's a dirty pile of broken-down ruins. The crookedness of its streets is matched only by that of the **local government**.

Rome's craziest site is **Vatican City**, a Catholic theme park complete with **people in funny costumes** who walk around waving.

---

[4]The French barbarian is known to archaeologists as Filet Magnon Man.

You can take pictures of them with your kids. And who's the leader of them all, that's made for you and me? **The pope**, who is sort of like a **king** in that he wears a **silly hat**. But do *not* make fun of this hat if you meet him, because the one difference between the king and the pope is that the pope has **fire and brimstone** at his disposal. We don't even know what brimstone is, but we're not asking.

The **Sistine Chapel** here has **pictures on the ceilings**, conveniently placed there to cover up the embarrassing stains behind them from the last papal party, held back in 1532 by **Pope Pius the Sloshed**.

 You should keep in mind their attitudes regarding punctuality and not offend their culture by doing things they would frown upon such as **showing up at places on time**. If, for example, you are invited to dinner at 6:00, then it would be considered rude to arrive any time before the following Thursday.

What this means for us is that **shops** and **restaurants** may not be open when we expect them to be, times like weekday afternoons, Sundays, and summer. Southern Italy is one of the few areas we encountered in which the restaurants close for lunch.

 ## Lamb, Lamb, Lamb: Play "One-Up"!

In this game you visit Europe's most impressive sights and loudly proclaim that they suck compared to things in the United States. Give yourself points for style, creativity, and sheer ignorance. For example:

At the Leaning Tower of Pisa: "This sucks! It's crooked! You want bad architecture? We had a whole office building *collapse* back in Connecticut a few years back! Beat that!" (6 points)

At the statue of David: "This sucks! He's naked and he's got no pupils! And he's enormous! Are you sure this isn't Goliath? Man, if we wanted to see big naked men, we'd've bought a copy of *Playgirl!* At least those are in *color!*" (8 points)

At the Sistine Chapel: "This sucks! Y'ever seen **Grand Central Station**? Yeah, they got pictures on the ceilings, and the ones there even glow in the dark! The Cis*tern* Chapel, that's what you oughta call *this* tub!" (10 points)

The last sight in the Vatican is **St. Peter's Basilica**, which is a big BIG **BIG** church. It makes any church in the U.S. look like a **Fisher-Price barn**, the kind with the door that moos whenever you open it. *Entire countries* make pilgrimages to this church, only to lose their way forever wandering inside its vast interior. If you come across **Latvia** while visiting, please inform the nearest guard.

Shorts and sleeveless T-shirts are not allowed inside the basilica, so please remove them before entering.

Outside of the Vatican you will find **ruins**. Walk east through these until you come to the ***ancient* ruins**, which will not appear as run-down. The most well known of these is the **Colisseum**, a symbol of ancient Rome's grandeur and culture because inside it they **slaughtered** thousands of **innocent people**. Descendants of these very Romans now get the same enjoyment from **soccer matches**. No doubt their forefathers would shake their heads in shame if they saw how far their boys had fallen.

Europe Close-Up: Soccer

European football is so dull and visionless that it actually involves *feet touching a ball,* as opposed to the innovative American version, which has almost nothing to do with its name.

The first thing you must realize is that you won't see any Giuseppe Montañas or Wilhelm "Der Kühlschrank" Perriers bashing heads overseas. Europeans are only trying to disguise their own sissy sport when they call it football. But don't be fooled. Europeans play **soccer**.

Yes, soccer. **Grown men** wear short shorts and kneepads, think up cool names for themselves like the Blue Strikers, and sit around a cooler munching orange slices at halftime.

You may suspect by now that European football doesn't quite have the same level of brute force, war-is-hell, rough-and-tumble, "Let's-roll-that-tape-of-Joe-Theisman's-shin-*one*-more-time," senseless, male-bashing-male, bloody violence that makes American football so appealing. But actually, their matches involve at least as much bloodletting. It's just not on the field.

The most dangerous position in a European soccer game is generally considered **center bleacher**. If you were planning to attend a game you may want to consider sticking to less dangerous places in Europe—Yugoslavia, for example.

Not even the loudest, drunkest, most beer-bellied American Bleacher Creature will prepare you for Europe. American fans have such cushy traditions as the **wave**, the **bullshit!** cheer, and the **four-hour-later-ballpark-frank belch**. European fans, on the other hand, join in games like the **chain-link-fence press**, the **collapsing bleacher**, and the **toddler trample**.

It's sad, really, that grown European fans can get themselves so worked up about a game that Americans generally outgrow by the time their voice changes. But **1994**, they thought, would change it all, because this was the year that the U.S.A. hosted the **World Cup**, the biggest competition on Earth named after a piece of protective equipment.

Teams arrived for the honor of playing soccer in the United States, and indeed had a unique experience, for they weren't used to playing in stadiums with **empty home team seats**.

SICILY

Si-*silly*! Don't let the big billboard ads that boast HOME OF THE MAFIA and BILLIONS AND BILLIONS SEVERED scare you off—Sicily is much more than that. We owe a lot to the Sicilians! And if we don't repay it by the end of the month, we'll lose a finger! No, just kidding! Sicilians, after all, are the folks who invented **square pizzas**, making this island sort of the Italian equivalent of **White Castle**.

Palermo

Palermo, also known as the City Whose Description Is Most Likely to Get Us Dropped to the **Bottom of the Ocean in Concrete Shoes**, is a quiet, rustic place, whose public buildings all exhibit a unique Swiss style of architecture. Swiss *cheese*, actually. Rat-a-tat-tat.

Sights

No matter how much you see in Palermo, it is important to realize that You Saw Nothing.

Most of the sights that you will Not See are within a few blocks of each other, interspersed with authentic Italian restaurants in which everyone is eating with their backs to the walls.

Whatever you do, be certain that you Didn't Go Near the **Palazzo dei Normanni**. It is from this perch that in the 1970s the mayor stood and declared a renewed war on the Mafia in his famous words, "No longer will we let this Mafia's reign of terror contin—aaiiieeeee!" Thus ended the renewed war on the Mafia.

Europe Close-Up: Corruption

People have tried for decades to figure out what the Mafia is all about. Now, because you bought this book, you're going to find out and be the life of the next cocktail party.

The Mafia isn't about power. It isn't about money, and it isn't about free pasta dinners. It's about one thing, and one thing only: **ugly fat guys trying to get laid**.

The Mafia was formed because a bunch of overweight pimple mongers with crooked noses couldn't get a date. So they went around terrorizing shopkeepers and collecting finger samples to look *macho*. That's right, it's just another Italian *machismo* thing. A lot of strutting and big talking *aaand* occasionally a wedding massacre or art museum bombing. But it's all a put-on.

Now they've got the babes, but Mafia people are still pulling the ol' "Meet me in an empty warehouse. . . . *Naaaah*, I ain't setting you up!" trick because they know something's missing. And do you know what that something is? They want to be **loved**! Just like you and me! That's why they're always hugging and kiss(of death)ing each other. So the next time you see some oatmeal-cookie-faced stoogie toting an elephant gun on his back, just walk up to him and give him a big, slurpy **smooch**! Tell him how great he looks! Make him feel *Mafio-so-sexy*! We can turn this crime ring into a circle of light with just a little love, and then we'll be one big happy Coke-commerical-and-Barney-the-dinosaur-watching world! *Capisce?*

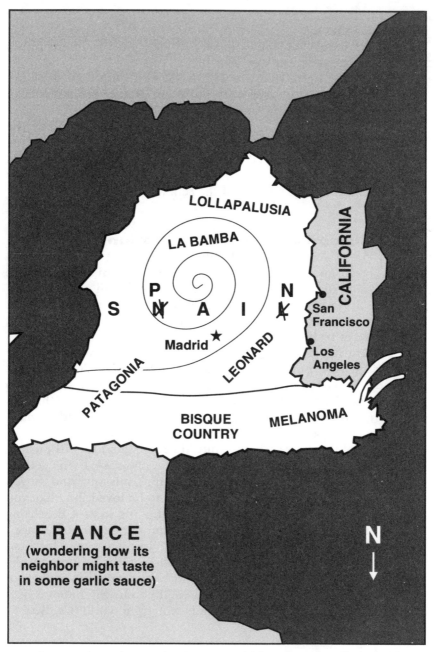

The mystery of Spain's slow-paced lifestyle is finally solved.

(S)pain
Land of the Los

How often while we were in Spain
Did we wish we were back on the plane?
Again and again and again and again
And again and again and again.

SPAIN
VITAL INFORMATION

Currency in use: The piñata

Dominant stereotype: Smoking, drinking, bull-fighting, flamenco-dancing, late-at-night-up-staying party-holics

Official motto: Motto? We don' need no steenkin' motto!

Theme song: "Tomorrow"

For fun: Running down narrow, dead-end streets with several large, massive horny creatures in hot pursuit[1]

Contributions to American culture: California city names

Ugly American visits, returns with: sombreros (*Olé!*), porcelain bulls (*Olé!*), the shits (*Olé!*)

Overall rating (−10 to 0): −5

How to sound like you've really, truly been there: "Sucked. The only traditional event I experienced was the Running of the Bowels."

Most Europeans tend to think of Spaniards the way recent Democratic presidents probably view their delinquent younger siblings: They're a little crude, a bit crazy, their beer sucks, and they're just not that funny, but you gotta love 'em anyway. The typical European view runs something like this: "Spain? Yeah, it's pretty cool for a **Third World country**."

History
If there's one thing the Spanish are, it's history.

Spanish history is particularly convenient because **everything happened in 1492**. Really. They got *all* their history out of the way in one year, and haven't bothered with it since. Here are some of the big events:

---

[1] bulls or males, depending on your sex

• **Columbus**, sponsored jointly by Spain and Pizza Hut, discovers America, which Europeans regard as an uncultured wasteland teeming with brutish, ill-mannered barbarians. Some opinions never change.

• **Juice** is expelled from the country. To this day, citrus fruits remain one of Spain's biggest exports.[2]

• **The Moors** finally leave after a 700-year occupation, and Queen Isabella tells Ferdinand she doesn't care how much fun they are, the Moors are *not* to be invited to their next party.

• A new era begins for "**Spanish Inquisition**." We are not sure, but we believe it must have been a wildly successful **game show** of that era.

Food
Spain has many wonderful regional dishes, like **salmonella** and **copacabana** and **placenta**. Order the sampler!

Practical Information
Lines: People do not form lines in Spain; they form enormous throbbing globs of disconnected limbs. It's a **German's nightmare**. In fact, in *all of Spain* there is only one line. It goes, "You are the most beautiful woman in the world. Will you care to be having with me a one night stand?"

Holidays: Every afternoon!

Transportation: They have a saying 'round here which you may have heard, "The train in Spain is waited for in vain." And hitchhikers *never* get picked up, except in bars.

Supermarkets: Orange.

Culture
Nothing quite captures the glory and vitality of Spanish culture like the **drag flamenco dancing shows** we accidentally walked into in Seville. But don't think that's all Spain has to offer!

---

[2]Correction: We have just been told that it was not juice, but **Jews** who were expelled from Spain in 1492. We apologize for this error. If you've ever been to Spain in 1492, then you know it wasn't exactly the Garden of Eden they were banished from.

Cervantes's epic ***Don Quixote*** is considered to be the Great American Novel in Spain, despite its not having a *single* gratuitous drag flamenco dancing scene. Instead, Cervantes weaves the tale of a deluded man who roams the Spanish countryside looking for windmills to attack, which proves he's crazy because everyone knows that windmills are in **Holland**.

Then there are the artists, from **Hello Dali**, who firmly believed "Time doesn't fly—it hangs from trees and melts!," to **Pablo Picasso**, who created a style of painting the human body best described as Cuisin art.

TYPICAL LATE PICASSO

 Understanding Those Peculiar Natives

If Spaniards ever made plans in advance, their typical plan-a-day calendar would look something like this:

	SUNDAY	MONDAY	TUESDAY	WEDNESDAY	THURSDAY	FRIDAY	SATURDAY
Day	siesta	siesta	siesta	siesta	labora	siesta	siesta
Night	fiesta	fiesta	fiesta	fiesta	fiesta	fiesta	fiesta

Spain by day is only slightly cooler than a toaster oven, so you can't blame them if they're too warm and sweaty to even procrastinate properly.

So they wait until night, and then they get all their procrastinating done—it's time to *"Sheque, sheque, sheque toyo booty!,"* as the old Spanish saying goes. One should exercise caution when partying with Spaniards, because they're a little crazier than what we're used to. If you're not careful, you could end up doing something stupid that you'll regret later, like **allowing yourself to be chased by bulls**.

THE BASQUE COUNTRY

The Basques are typical Spaniards in that they would rather be fried up in a *paella* dish and served up to a group of snotty French tourists than be called typical Spaniards.

 ### Sights
This area has many wonderful cultural features such as **political unrest**, but don't worry! According to one hardly competing guidebook, "your chances of being caught up in political violence are far less likely than those of being robbed in New York. . . ."

Well now! Since only **70 percent of all tourists** in New York get robbed,[3] what's there to worry about? But enough about Basque 'n' robbin'.

Pamplona
Every year Pamplona's week-long party, La Fiesta de San Fermín (the Party of Saint Vermin), is the site of the famous **Running of the Bulls**. The only comparable event here in the U.S. is every four years, when we have *two* parties who partake in the famous **Running of the Bullshitters**. But why get political?

Europe Close-Up: The Running of the Bulls
The Running of the Bulls is *not* what happens when the bulls drink the water in southern Spain. No, it is the traditional way for thousands of young males to prove they are real men by doing something **incredibly stupid**. Folks here party in the streets all night, drunk and happy and overturning cars on police officers in celebration.[4] From up above, old women **throw water** on everyone

---

[3]This figure does not include the 25 percent who get killed.
[4]Pamplona Bulls fans apparently have a little too much in common with their Chicago Bulls counterparts.

below, shouting a cheer which we assume translates to something like, "Wake up, you idiots! You're about to get gored through your backside!"

Finally, at 8:00 A.M. the bulls are released upon the runners as well as anyone who passed out in the street the night before, and spectators can watch the complete show within minutes:

Fast Runners: Waaaaaaaagh! [Runrunrun]

Average Runners: WAAAAAaaaaagh!! [Runrunrunrunrun]

Bulls: [Clompclompclomp] Snort, snort! [Clomp]

Slow Runners:
[Ahem]

Slow Runners:

Uh . . . Slow Runners?:

Considering ourselves typically small-brained, large-testicled males, we decided to join in the fun. Just before it started, however, we experienced what you might call the **running of the balls**, and slunk off into the sidelines, sissies but safe.

LA COSTA BRAVA

La Costa Brava is a scenic country in the northeast of Spain whose warm, luscious Mediterranean beaches you may or may not be able to barely glimpse in between all **those nutty Germans** on vacation who got up at 5 A.M. to claim the best spots. But don't worry, it's not *all* Germans here! No, there are some **British**, too, who've come here to relax a little and work on their burn.

Barcelona

The revered patron saint of the city of Barcelona is **Saint Cobi**. Cobi, you recall, was the **official rat of the 1992 Summer Olympics**, who united the nations of the world as they gathered for the competition known as:

> **"What the bejingles kind of animal**
> ***is* that, anyway?"**[5]

---

[5]Winners: U.S.A. got the bronze with the entry "a squirrel," Unified Washed-Up World Power Team won the silver for "a rat," and the Germans took the gold with their answer, "Who cares?"

It was only after Atlanta revealed *their* mascot for 1996[6] that everyone scratched their heads and decided Cobi wasn't really all that bad after all.

COBI, THE 1992 OLYMPIC MASCOT

 ## Europe Close-Up: The Olympics

Every four years the world converges on a designated city to litter its sidewalks, deface its sights, shout nationalist taunts at its citizens, pee in its alleyways, and leave it with a mongo construction debt from which it rarely ever recovers. The cities of the world consider this a great honor and compete for the glory of hosting this event, known as the **Summer Olympics**.

Barcelona was the most recent sucker, and this was a very special Olympics, not only because **Cobimania** reigned in the streets, not only because it was the *last time* them Commies would beat our medal count, but also because it was the first time there was an **Official Olympic Pin Trading Center** in town, which was great because it kept all the **geeks** in one area of the city. Pinheads from around the world gathered at the **Official Olympic Pin Trading Center** to exchange pins and then stick them all over their hats and jackets, because of course everyone knows that one's ability to

---

[6]It was named Whatthefreakizit? by the winners of the Name Our Mascot Based on Your Initial Reaction Contest. Runners up included Boyizithideous, Itlookzliketheelephantsmurf, Haroldizthatyou? and AAAAAAaaaaaaahhhhh!

attract members of the opposite sex is directly proportional to how many hundreds of individual Cobi pins one is able to display on one's clothing.

Right now you're probably wondering, "What kind of Beanie-Weenie-brain would do this?" Well, all we have to say is that if you call our **dad** a Beanie-Weenie-brain one more time, you're in for it. Yes, *dad.* We can't say that we're proud, but at least he's not collecting Franklin Mint Star Trek chess sets or anything like that.

 ## Sights

"One life is not enough for Barcelona," said one comedian who got plenty of laughs. Barcelona's only sight is the **Temple Expiatori de la Sagrada Família Zenyatta Mondatta Inigo Montoya Solo Para Uso Externo**, a bizarre sand-drip castle church, which if you stare at it long enough has the amazingly remarkable ability to make you certain you must be on a bad acid trip, even if you've never taken LSD in your entire life.

Do not visit this church. It is far and away the **second most frightening thing in all of Europe**.[7] And when it's *not* far and away but up close and personal, it gets even scarier. Numerous tourists have had the unfortunate experience of **turning to stone** upon seeing this monster. We feel we should warn you we checked and turning to stone is *not covered* by most travel insurance plans. Of all of Gaudi's efforts, there's no doubt this is the Gaudiest.

---

[7]See "food" under Germany.

MADRID

If we had roads,
they would all lead to Madrid.
    —One Smart Spaniard

History

Up until the seventies, Spain had a dictator named **Franco**, a man despised by much of the Spanish population because his name meant "French." Franco's personal influence, however, suffered a significant decline following his **death** in 1975. Democracy was soon declared, and the Spanish have been out **partying** in celebration ever since.

MAP OF DOWNTOWN MADRID

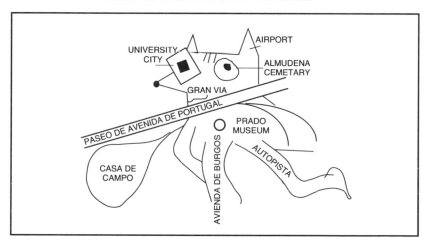

Food

We were *very* excited to hear that everyone in Spain goes to **topless bars**, so we hopped right on the next plane, traveled 7,000 miles, and imagine our disappointment when we arrived in Madrid and found out that it's **tapas bars** that everyone goes to.

    Tapas are Spanish snacks much like **pasta**, but all mixed up. Different bars serve different tapas, which you can wash down with the famous **Madrid cider shower**. Helpful locals tell tourists that the traditional way to drink cider is to—yeah, yeah—have it poured by a waitress from two feet above your mouth. This is the main source of entertainment for the helpful locals.

 ## Europe Close-Up: The Great European Smoke-Out

Europeans are *all* smokaholics. Happy? Have a cigarette. Sad? Have a cigarette. Just finished a cigarette? Congratulations, have a cigarette! About to have a cigarette? How about a warm-up smoke? Just passed the first grade? Here . . .

Europeans know SMOKING IS COOL! Philip Morris, Joe Camel, and the Marlboro Man are regarded as something of a Holy Trinity over here. **Lung cancer** is actually a status symbol in Europe; there's no surer way of impressing the opposite sex[8] than by flashing your **tracheotomy club** card and suavely asking, "Sssssoh. . . . Hack, hack. Come hhhhhhhere offffffften? Hack, hack."

A large body of mythology has built up around the legendary quest for **a nonsmoking section** in Europe, but no sightings have ever been confirmed. Even surgeons have been known to light up in the operating room ("Rico, stop flicking your ashes in the aorta"). Spaniards in particular have contributed more than their share in reducing the ozone layer. You'll quickly be labeled a noodle head (*cabeza con pasta*) if you're not either puffing on a cigar or trembling vigorously.

Practical Information

Following are the most important phrases one will need in Madrid and the rest of Spain:

- **Hey, waiter! This rice is yellow!** *¡Jey, camarero! ¡Este arroz está amarillo!*

- **Well, since you can't explore the New World anymore, I'm glad to see you're making do with my back pocket.** *¡Váyase! ¡Váyase!*

- **You have a very strange French dialect in these parts.** ·*Usted tiene un dialecto frogés muy extraño en estas partes.*

---

[8]besides wearing a jacket covered with Olympics pins, that is

• **Hey! Where's the flippin' toilet? All I see is this hole in the floor!** *¡Jey! ¿Dónde está el servicio flipando? ¡Todo veo es éste hoyo en el piso!*

• **What the hell do you mean, "Squat"?** *¿Qué el infierno quiere decir usted, "Como un Sumo"?*

Europe Close-Up: Tourist Language Books

The average pocket language book attempts to condense the lingual needs of the average Ugly American into about 150 pages, as if the average Ugly American really ever uses any phrase besides, "English? You speak English?"

The *Don't Go: Europe! Pocket Language Guide* would be a significant improvement because it would only be three pages long, and you could use the same book for *any* foreign language, *even British*. It would look something like this:

DON'T GO: EUROPE'S POCKET LANGUAGE GUIDE

AT THE TRAIN STATION

When you want to know when a train leaves:	"English? ENGLISH! WHEN! DOES! THIS! TRAIN! LEAVE?"

AT THE RESTAURANT

When you don't know what a certain item is on the menu:	"English? ENGLISH! WHAT! THE! HELL! IS! THIS! ITEM! ON! THE! MENU? IT'S! NOT! A! FROG! IS! IT? GEEZ! CAN'T! YOU! FRRNERS! JUST! LEARN! ENGLISH! LIKE! THE! REST! OF! US?"
When you're ready to order:	"English? ENGLISH! I WANT *UN* BIG MAC! *POR FAFOR!*"

AT THE DISCO

When you want to meet someone:	"English? ENGLISH! WAIT! WHERE! ARE! YOU! GOING?"

The *Don't Go: Europe! Pocket Language Guide* would recommend learning only **two words** before visiting another country. But these are two very important words, essential if you are to maintain any shred of dignity while visiting a foreign land. These two vital words are

PUSH and PULL

But in today's inefficient ***Berlitz*** guidebooks, you will not see these words until *page 155*, by which time you will already have learned such phrases as "The washbasin is clogged," "I am expecting some money from Chicago," and "I'd like some acne cream, please."

Our two favorite *Berlitz* sections are

• The **dating/picking up skanky foreigners section**. This has phrases like "May I take you home?" that you can suavely try out on someone and then **grin dumbly** because you have no idea what their answer means.

• The **emergency section**, conveniently located in the **middle of the book** on page 156. Deep in here one can find the phrase "STOP, THIEF."

DON'T GO'S FUN QUIZ

Someone has just snatched your pocketbook and is running off through the crowd. The logical thing to do is
  a) chase him.
  b) yell "Stop!," since Spaniards have all watched enough American cop shows to know what it means.
  c) Whoa, pardner! Slow down! Fish out your **language guidebook**.[9] Next, take a few minutes to flip through it until you find "STOP, THIEF." Be patient! Now, after reading the pronunciation guide a few times so you can say it properly, yell "DETENTE, LADRON!" so that the thief, who by this time is halfway to Waikiki on a boat purchased with your travelers' checks, knows exactly who you're talking to.

If you picked letter c, then you're a **fool**, because you're wrong!
Even if you did manage to know the phrase or find it in time, your foreign accent will be so bad that most folks will end up pointing you to the nearest acne cream store instead.

---

[9]assuming it wasn't in your pocketbook

ANDALUSIA

Andalusia is the southern part of Spain, filled with people whom you should refer to as **Andalusers**. They have a popular tradition here of naming their cities after **large American cars**, for example: Seville and Granada.

Seville

Seville is best known for hosting the **World's Fair-to-Middlin'** in 1992, in which it gamely competed with Barcelona in accumulating the **biggest debt** in a limited amount of time.

Sights

The great thing we discovered about Seville is that you can simply walk right into any old cabaret off the street, sit down, smile at the ladies performing traditional Spanish dances as they mischievously wink at you, loosen your tie, kick back, and after fifteen minutes of music and bold flirtation realize that you're watching a **drag flamenco dancing show**. Then you can shift uncomfortably in your seat for a while, trying your best to act as if all along you had *intended* to be watching a drag flamenco dancing show, and finally scuttle out at the first intermission, visibly relieved. Not that this happened to us.

On your way out, snap some pics of the **banana-suited street cleaners**, who are paid by the state to sit on the sidewalk and guard the trash there.

Seville is also home to the famous Teenage Mutant Gothic Cathedral, a *sicko-big* church underneath which is the **Tumba de Cristóbal Colón** (Tomb of Christopher's Colon).

Europe Close-Up: The High Life

American tourists attach great importance to visiting every city's token tall monument, climbing up, and viewing the roofs of all the buildings—as if by peeking in on someone's long underwear flapping in the wind they'll get a better feel for the culture of a city.

To understand this, one must first realize the "masculine" role that Americans play toward other countries. Technical, obstinate, physically protective yet at the same time completely boneheaded, America has always assumed a stereotypically male character in its dealings with the world. Thus, when Americans visiting another country spot what might be a symbol of masculinity (The Eiffel

Tower, Big Ben, or, acknowledging that Italian culture has passed its climax, the Leaning Tower of Pisa), they feel compelled to visit it, climb to the top, and once there exclaim in a loud voice, "WELL, THIS IS A PRETTY TALL ONE, I GUESS. . . . BUT NOT AS BIG AS THE ONES WE'VE GOT BACK IN THE STATES!" This is usually enough to comfort the American about the relative size of his monuments.

Entertainment

Do you like watching **animals being killed**? Boy, do we have a treat for you! **Bullfights** are popular events in which crowds gather to cheer on men and shout "Olé!" as they **slaughter innocent animals for fun**.

And what brave men they are! First they let the bull loose and run him around the stadium 'til he's tired. Run, run, *runrunrun- runrunrunrun*.

Now the bull's steamed. He walks around giving mean Billy Idol sneers to the crowd, and his **testicles**, which hang **almost to the ground** and could be used for the **hammer throw**, swing *baaack* and forth, *baaack* and forth, *swingswingswingswingswing*. This is one badass bull.

Then the bull-killers-in-training, known as **cuspidors**, come in on horses and **stab the bull** in the back, **stab the bull** in the back, *stabstabstabstabstab* as they pass, supposedly only enough to make it angry, although this particular kind of anger seems to involve a lot of stumbling and disorientation.

Finally, the **extremely brave matador** steps out, does a little tango around the dying bull, twirls a red cape in front of it as the bull uses its last energy to hobble towards it, and **stabs the bull** one last time right through the neck, *stabstabstabstabstab*, putting it out of its misery.

By the end of the show, if you're like most tourists, you'll probably find yourself **rooting for the bull**. We were hoping it would do enough tromping to make a **doramat** out of the matador.

We here at *Don't Go* feel one should only kill animals if there's a pressing reason for it—say, to make **McNuggets**. Thus, we would like to see a gradual phasing out of bullfighting to be replaced by the much more civilized display of **chickenfighting**. One could keep all the customs and rituals in place, but just release a **chicken** into the arena instead of a bull for the matador to kill. This would be just as entertaining, and much more ethical.

Granada

Granada has recovered remarkably since our **invasion** in 1986. It seems, based on our interviews, that most people have forgotten that it ever happened at all.

Granada is home to the famous **Gypsy caves**, where you can meet and be swindled by **real Gypsies**! ("Ah, I see your fortune now. . . . I'm taking your fortune. . . . I'm adding it to my own fortune. . . . Here's the embassy number, kid. Hope you find a way home.")

 ## Europe Close-Up: Gypsies!

The **Gypsies'** name is derived from the two words *gyp*, as in "They'll *gyp* you out of half your money," and *sies*, as in "They'll forcibly *sies* the rest of it." Sure, they've taken a lot of persecution, but they've also taken a lot of purses.

Gypsy Territory is anywhere in southern or eastern Europe, fairly congruous with Decreased Productivity Territory or Can't Get *U.S.A. Today* Territory or "What's That Grody Smell?" Territory.

They've developed all sorts of **scams** to bilk you out of your savings:

The not-so-great train robbery: Someone throws **sleeping gas** into your train compartment, knocking you out while they grab your belongings. Got your money in a neck pouch, you clever lug? Never fear, they'll **cut right through your shirt** to get it!

The low-down **Trading Places** *scenario:* Two folks will plant an illegal drug on you, and then threaten to turn you in unless, of course, you can think of a way to change their minds. . . .

The ol' "throw the baby at the tourists" trick: A Gypsy woman will literally *throw her baby* at you, and when you let go of everything to catch it, grab your suitcase and wallet, if it's still intact by that time of day.

The best way to avoid them? Don't Go!

SEPARATED AT BERN?

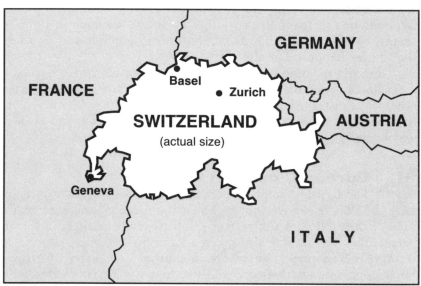

Gold-dealing Switzerland . . .

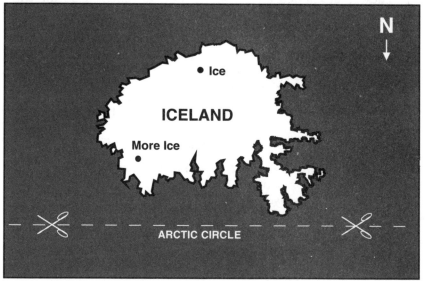

and cold-feeling Iceland

Switzzzzzzzzzz . . . erland

Quiet, please! Be calm and cautious.
Noise and kids and fun are banned.
That's okay—we've got cool watches!
Welcome, folks, to Switzerland.

SWITZERLAND
VITAL INFORMATION

Currency in use: Mine, all of mine. They ripped me off for every Swiss franc I had.

Dominant stereotype: Rich, politically impotent, cheese-eating neat-freaks

Official motto: All major credit cards accepted

Theme Song: "Fondue, Fondue, Fondue ('Til Her Daddy Takes the Cheese Pot Away)"

For fun: Co-ed, naked international banking

Contributions to American culture: cool army knives, the Heidi series (*Heidi, Heidi Come Home, Heidi III: The Revenge, Heidi Goes Bananas, Heidi: The Joys of Being a Woman*)

Ugly American visits, returns with: new Swatch, year's supply of hot chocolate mix, uncontrollable urge to spit on the sidewalk without being jailed.

Overall rating (scale of −10 to 0): −4

How to sound like you've really, truly been there: "Uh! I'll never be able to eat this *American* cheese again!"

All right, Switzerland, Land of Switzer, is not exactly a really, really big country. You could probably jog around it. But it *is* really, really big-*headed*, a nation of Switz Twits, so we feel a deep obligation to skewer them anyway.

Let's Go: Europe informs us that "Switzerland is ... more staid than spectacular." *Let's Go: Europe* is being extremely tactful. Switzerland is ... **boring**.

How boring? Let's just say there's boring, and then there's *borrrring*. Switzerland happens to be both. Boring like the Atomic Clock Channel. Boring like Faulkner. Boring like solitaire Parcheesi. A veritable 10 on the bore-ometer! This is why Swiss **clocks** and **watches** are so world-famous—not because they're better than others, but 'cause when people are in Switzerland all they do is stare at them, waiting for time to pass.

OK, sure, the **scenery**—lakes, mountains, villages, village lakes, mountain villages, mountain lakes, lakey mountains, mountainous lakey village mountain lakes—can be spectacular in between yawns. So we'll give in a little: Switzerland can be a great place to **take a nap** outside.

Sights
- lakes
- mountains
- villages

Entertainment
Tick, tock, tick, tock . . .

History
Switzerland has spent centuries perfecting its own brand of bland. A few years ago was the **700th anniversary** of the last recorded time anyone admitted having fun here and the country's founding, when a few kingdoms got together and promised to cooperate on things like **military defense**, **political rule**, and gypping the average supermarket customer by putting **air holes in the cheese** and convincing everyone that it's a sign of quality.

At this time appeared Switzerland's most famous hero and only known contribution to history, **William Tell**, whose exploits with his band of merry men, stealing from the rich and giving to the poor, have become legendary in America and other countries that can't tell him apart from Robin Hood. As we recall the legend, the sheriff of Nottingham forced William Tell to shoot an apple off his son's head, thus discovering gravity.

For some time after this, Switzerland was your run-of-the-mill land-hungry, war-mongering, meat-eating, NRA-supporting country. Around 1515, however, the same enemies that Switzerland had previously been using as sausage filler started ganging up on them, forcing the Swiss to unleash upon them their Top Secret Amazingly Devious Emergency Wartime Strategy:

"Waitwaitwait! Time out! We're *neutral!*"

From that day on the **Swiss Army** gave up fighting and instead turned to the much more important task of making **knives with built-in nose hair clippers**.

Since then, Switzerland has remained exactly the same.

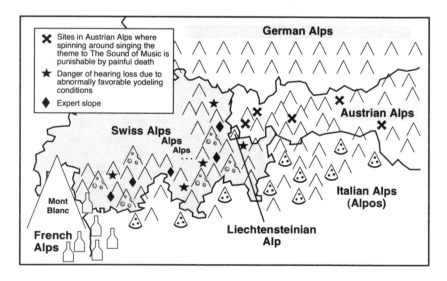

Culture

Contrary to widespread belief, Swiss cultural influence goes far beyond **Swatches** and **cheese**. For example, there's **Heidi**, a cute little mountain girl who's always doing crazy things like **preempting pro football games**, for which most Americans would like to thank her by giving her an **army knife** to go play with, preferably one of those ultra-deluxe models with a built-in circular saw and welding iron and hot-air popcorn popper. America is also indebted to Switzerland for some of its most prized figures, most notably that little **yodeling mountain-climber guy on "The Price Is Right."**

Switzerland is also the big, wishy-washy neutrality, the Judge Wapner of international relations. Of course the Cold War is over; Switzerland now plays the dubious role of a neutrality in a world where *everyone else is on the same team*. But those Swiss are sticking to their knives and staying neutral. That's what we call real spunk, and boy we wish we were more like the Swiss, although not if we have to wear those silly leather pants.

TOPILLOGICAL MAP OF THE ALPS

✖ Sites in Austrian Alps where spinning around singing the theme to The Sound of Music is punishable by painful death

★ Danger of hearing loss due to abnormally favorable yodeling conditions

◆ Expert slope

German Alps

Austrian Alps

Swiss Alps
Alps
Alps
. . .

Italian Alps
(Alpos)

Mont Blanc

Liechtensteinian Alp

French Alps

GENEVA

History

In Geneva meet two of Europe's most famous cultures: the chocolate-eating Swiss of the east, and the coffee-drinking French of the west. The founding of this city from just a poop-ridden deer path in the woods is a favorite legend, often acted out at civic events:

[Two travelers bump into each other]
Frenchman: "Ooof! You've got your chocolate in my coffee!"
Swissman: "You've got your coffee on my chocolate!"
Both: "MMMMmmmmmm. . . . Tastes great! Let's build a city!"
Frenchman: "Right here!"
Swissman: "On this poop-ridden deer path!"

Never underestimate the powers of **mocha**, folks.

Sights

While in Geneva you will want to check out the **big artificial geyser** in the middle of the lake, erected there to mark the **Tomb of the Unknown Bidet**. The Swiss were their usual creative selves in naming this landmark, finally settling upon the **Jet of Water**. It has become the most famous symbol of this city, forever beckoning to its visitors, "Come to Geneva, and you'll leave with a clean rump!" The Jet of Water makes Geneva the only city in the world to claim an **open fire hydrant** as its biggest attraction.

Geneva is also host to the **United Nations**, a large association of translators who have adopted a diplomat from each country and occasionally put them all in the same room to see what happens.[1]

Europe Close-Up: The United Nations

The United Nations is an organization designed to unite all the bureaucrats of the world, thus keeping them out of everyone else's hair. They have a famous recipe here for **peace treaties**. At the onset of any crisis, UN delegates are lightning-quick to respond by squabbling amongst themselves for weeks and weeks and weeks and weeks behind closed doors, finally coming out with

---

[1]answer: not much

a resolution in hand which firmly states that all parties had better cease fighting *immediately*, or else the delegates threaten to go back behind those same closed doors and squabble for a few weeks more about what to do next. By the time any action is agreed upon, the countries in question usually have ceased to exist, whether through mutual annihilation or the natural shift of the continents.

Occasionally the UN will send out an international[2] peacekeeping[3] force,[4] but things always seem to fall apart when the Belgians start complaining that the Germans are hogging the cots and when the French refuse to eat what the English mess captain has meticulously overboiled for them.

Entertainment

Geneva is considered **diverse** in Switzerland, which means to them that it has both filthy-rich **bankers** *and* filthy-rich **bureaucrats**—multicultural for multimillionaires. The average age in this city is comparable to that of **crude oil**. The whole city shuts down at 5 P.M.; by 5:15, the place is swept, the lights are out, and a little man in overalls has shuffled out to the highway exit ramp and flipped the WELCOME sign over to CLOSED.

Accommodations

University housing. A popular option in many cities, where you can relive your glorious college days, sleeping in a dank broom closet on bare springs with one or more roommates who pursue "alternative hygienic lifestyles."

Our parents', Route Malagnou. Free accommodations, excellent food, and cable TV in a central location. You'll have to help with the dishes, though, as well as put up with constant nagging about just what you are going to do with your life, anyway.

BASEL

Note: *During the time that we spent in Basel, it was a Sunday and did not stop raining, which prevented us from actually leaving the train station. However, we feel that this should not affect our providing an honest, objective account of Basel's main sights and*

---

[2]American
[3]war-making
[4]force

attractions. We proudly present our review heretohenceforthwith:

Upon arrival, one is struck by both the cramped size and dirty, train-station feel of Basel. Everything is gray and dirty, the shops are closed, and frankly we felt more like we were in a **Greyhound Bus terminal** than a European city.

Fortunately, everything is centrally located, and one can see all the main sights within the space of an hour-long layover—as we did.

 ## Sights

The city of Basel offers many sights. We found a **candy shop**, two **newsstands**, and a small **fruit market**. Try the peaches!

Basel's most popular landmark is the **ticket window**, a bustling attraction on the north side of the city which boasts all the trappings of an authentic place to purchase tickets. Come early, though; the line gets long during the afternoon hours.

Stroll down the main pedestrian ramp, under the warm, urine yellow lights of the Basel station, admiring the years of accumulated **dust and dirt** perched along its sides, and only then will you truly know this City of the Rising Fare. And if you're lucky enough to find an English speaker among the **vagrants and winos** that dot this city, he can provide you with hours of stimulating conversation as well.

To get away from all the hustle and bustle, make an excursion to the **restroom**.

 ## Europe Close-Up: European Restrooms

Homesick Americans will be pleased to discover that **public restrooms** in Europe are just as smelly and hair-infested as the ones back home. The one difference is that outside of all European public toilets, you'll see a **large old woman in light blue** sitting at a table, whose job it apparently is to sit there and make sure that no one comes in to clean them.

For this service, one is supposed to tip her a certain amount of money, depending on the amount and consistency of relief experienced. In theory this is optional, but most of these women bear a striking resemblance to **Kathy Bates** in *Misery*, so we suggest erring on the side of generosity.

BE BOLD! BE STUPID! BE AMERICAN!

The next time you find yourself facing such a tip plate,
toss in a handful of **American pennies**
with a big, cheerful **smile**.
Chances are she won't know the difference.

Food

Fortunately, **McDonald's** is just a block and a half from the station, so one need not go far outside the city for good food.

Europe Close-Up: European McDonald's

European McDonald's restaurants are the net result of the **Marshall Plan**, according to which the Americans promised to rebuild Europe after World War II on the condition that half the new buildings be good places to get a burger. Today they serve as miniature American colonies from which, God willing, we will one day take over the entire continent, turning all of its citizens into monosyllabic, hamburger-eating, overweight, grungy skateboarders. This wouldn't be such an important goal of ours if we didn't get such a kick out of pissing off the French.

ZURICH

Thousands of young Americans flock to Zurich every year, eager to see it for themselves after reading in *Let's Go* that it is "the quintessential banker's town."

History

Zurich's tremendous historical importance simply cannot be denied. Most recently, according to *Let's Go,*

**"James Joyce died of an ulcer
here in 1941."**

Well now! That must have been quite a headline-snatching year for this city, considering all that was happening anywhere else at the time was, oh, **World War II**.

Sights

Churches and museums have infected Zurich as well, but for something *really* modern and cutting-edge, make a pilgrimage to the **site of James Joyce's death**, who, by the way, **died of an ulcer** there in 1941.

Culture

If cleanliness is next to godliness, then Zurich is doing the Watusi with St. Peter. This place makes Disney World look like Dickens World. Although many cities boast that on a hot day you could fry an egg on their sidewalks, in Zurich you could fix an entire onion-and-cheese omelette, broil toast in a mailbox, squeeze fresh orange juice into a nearby ashtray, and down the whole meal using the daily paper to wipe your face, all without once worrying about cooties.

Before removing your shoes and entering the city, be sure to review the entrance sign:

> **WELCOME TO ZURICH**
> **"A REAL BANKER'S TOWN"**
> **—GERM-FREE SINCE 1868—**
> **—JAMES JOYCE-FREE SINCE 1941—**
> **LITTERING, SPITTING, SWEARING,**
> **SMOKING, SWEATING, SMELLING,**
> **SNEEZING, WIPING YOUR NOSE**
> **ON A SHIRT SLEEVE,**
> **PICKING YOUR EAR,**
> **SPLASHING AROUND THE TOILET RIM,**
> **CHEWING WITH YOUR MOUTH OPEN,**
> **AND LEAVING SMALL TOENAIL**
> **CLIPPINGS ON THE CARPET**
> **STRICTLY PROHIBITED**

This uptight attitude has taken a toll on many of Zurich's citizens, most notably **James Joyce**, who **died of an ulcer** there in 1941.

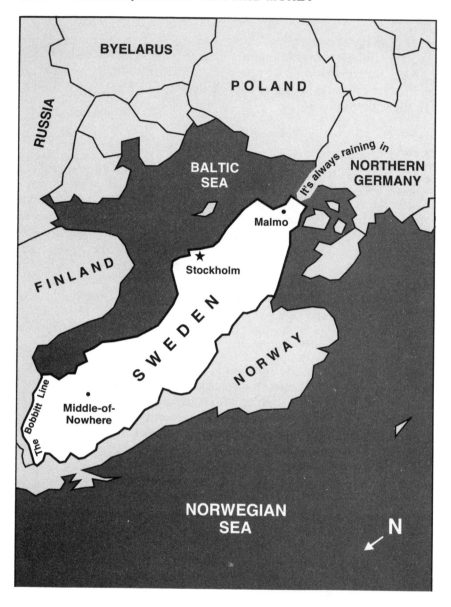

Healthy, robust Sweden is, many say, the shape of things to come.

Sveden
Land of Elk and Money

Because the sex is freer here,
Few folks do prostitate.
The only red light district near
Is Rudolph on your plate.

BUT FIRST, A WORD ABOUT SCANDINAVIA

Scandinavia is an elite group of large, phallic-shaped countries that exist primarily to supply the main continent below them with fresh cod, reindeer meat, schmaltzy pop groups, and the wind-chill factor.

Americans seem to think of all Scandinavians as **sex-crazed horn dogs**, as nothing but gorgeous, virile young men and women whom, they say, "make me wanna shoop." This gross generalization is both narrow-minded and unfair to Scandinavians, although we here at *Don't Go* also happen to believe that it is fairly accurate. We took one look around, saw that telltale healthy glow on all the citizens, the true sign of a liberated libido, and thought, "Is this *Scandinavia*, or *Randinavia*?"

But enough of the nasty. We don't mean to sound as if we're obsessed with sex or anything. So in the following chapter we will discuss—without once mentioning sex—the other aspects of Scandinavian life, just to show that we're not fixated with the sex lives of Scandinavians. Because we're not. Even if it is free and open unlike we've ever experienced before . . . with beautiful people well versed in the secret arts of erotica . . . and no worries about commitment . . . and long, sensual "Swedish massages" during breaks . . . and leftover meatballs in the morning. . . . Excuse us while we take a cold shower.

Thank you. We now proudly present Sweden, our token Scandinavian country.

SWEDEN

SWEDEN
VITAL INFORMATION

Currency in use: The b—Er, *kr*onor

Dominant stereotype: Blond, ruddy-faced, alcoholic health nuts with big smiles on their faces

Official motto: "We're not the cheese people!"

Theme song: "Take a Chance on Me"

For fun: Border wars with Norway

Contributions to American culture: Minnesota; the Swedish Chef, Wally Walrus, and other artificial Swedeners

Ugly American visits, returns with: Meatballs!

Overall rating (−10 to 0): −4

How to sound like you've really, truly, been there: "Heebee horbee dorbee svedee svordee svadee habee!"

The first thing you'll notice upon entering Sweden is that you've made an **enormous mistake**. Understand, they're wonderful people, even if they did eat Prancer, but they live in a very large, very empty **Frigidaire**.

Practical Information
Bring a sweater. And button up that coat. You'll catch your death.

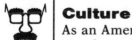

Culture
As an American unfamiliar with the national psyche, you may be puzzled as to why the normally friendly Swedes seem to **hate your guts**. Well, it's not for the usual reason natives

hate us (our collective Ugly American Tourist IQ). Swedes are actually pretty accommodating to idiots. They have to be; their entire tourism industry depends on them.[1]

But even if you changed your Hawaiian shirt, disposed of your disposable camera, got that finger out of your nose, and stopped making fuuun of the vay they taaalked, they would *still* hate you. Why? It's that grudge they still hold against us. You know, the way we never really took **ABBA** all that seriously? They hate that.

It was kinda cute of Sweden to try and create their own little band, but their best effort, **ABBA**, had all the hard, cutting edge of a Koosh ball. Ours, my friend, is the Real Man's side of the Atlantic, the side that produced Stallone and MX missiles and "Studs," and we don't drink tea or watch soccer or play accordions or anything like that over here, but most importantly we don't listen to that Eurosynth-pop schmaltz that Europeans call music, so we weren't *about* to "take a chance on" ABBA. But somehow ABBA tricked us with subversive *melodies* (how passé!) in their songs, the kind that drill deeper into your head the harder you try to forget them, the likes of which we hadn't heard since Captain and Tenille's "Love Will Keep Us Together." There's only one word for songs like that, and that word is **communist**.

 Subversive message in the music! Do you realize that if you play ABBA backwards . . . it's still ABBA?

ABBA *did* have one thing in common with all good rock groups, and that is this: they were **way ugly**. One look at this fearsome foursome, and you *know* why they didn't survive into the music video era.

By the start of the '80s, thinly disguised ABBA clones—Blondie, the Go-Go's, Soft Cell, Dexy's Midnight Runners, Toto, Asia, YAZ— had taken over our radios. But just when it all looked lost, along

---

[1]Typical Swedish tourist brochures promise "Come to Sweden! It's *really cold!*"

came our musical **Sigourney Weaver**, known as **rap**, blasting these ABBA aliens to pieces.

Meanwhile, Sweden was busy at the drum machine concocting a new, more powerful Son of ABBA. Unleashed to the world in the late '80s with their album *Look Sharp! Who Cares How We Sound?* was **Roxette**.

With the advent of Roxette and now the lovable **Ace of Base**, Sweden has finally overtaken its Swiss cousin as Europe's largest exporter of cheese.

STOCKHOLM

Pretty **buildings**, cobblestone **streets**, gothic **churches** . . . does this sound at *all* familiar to you? Stockholm takes all the regular features of a regular city and adds to it the Amazingly Remarkable "Alice, You Gotta See This!" Wonder:

cold snow

It's visible during **most of the year**, even at **night** because things never get completely dark up here, thanks to Sweden's unique position on the globe in an area known as . . . **Downwind of Chernobyl**.

Stockholm is also "not!"-able because it's a day and a half out of the way from any other—wait, let's rephrase that—from *any* place of interest in Europe. Thus one common characteristic of those who visit Stockholm is that they're **extremely lost**.

 ### History

Stockholm, according to this here almanac, was founded by Birger Jarl, a man whom, if he was half as interesting as his name sounds, was half of zero interesting. The Jarlster later went on to develop Sweden's first fast-food joint, Big Bob's World-Famous **Jarlbirgers** and Dasher Dogs.

Sights

Cold snow: Roll it! Pack it! Mold it into thousands of shapes! Hit your sister with it! Tromp around in it! Lose your way in it! Start to freeze in it! Cover yourself with it, trying to keep warm until someone finds you! Lose hope in it as night falls! Try to stay awake in it, but slowly drift off and never wake up! You'll never go back to your old terrain again!

The Riksbank: Described in many a guidebook as "one of the oldest **bank buildings** in the world," this is considered a major attraction in Stockholm. Be afraid. Be very afraid.

Grossland Estate and Museum: Home and memorial to ABBA, millions of Europeans make their annual pilgrimage here to pay tribute to these Europop gods. Hundreds of aging, overweight spinsters who've spent years listening to their ABBA discs, lighting candles at their personal ABBA shrines, and dreaming that ABBA will someday return and, upon seeing how faithful and good they have been, ask for their hand in marriage, fall to their pudgy knees as they approach the hallowed tomb of ABBA. . . . But is ABBA really dead? Down on the main continent, rumors of ABBA sightings still abound.

MALMO

Ask someone to describe the city of Malmö, and if there's one word they'll use, it's, "**Where?**"

Malmö is a small, modern city located in the reservoir tip area of Sweden.

 Sights
Besides the **Rooseum**, a collection of art that uses Astrospeak to disguise its true, evil identity ("Ret's go to the rooseum, Reorge!"), Malmö has two other attractions ("attraction" being a liberal, ballpark approximation). One is the **carriage museum**, which to us sounds only slightly more appealing than a **miscarriage museum** would be. The other physical attraction, according to a noncompetitive guidebook "southwest of the Stortorg is the attractive Lilla Torg." Well, you can imagine how miserable poor Lilla is these days, what with all these tourists banging down her door trying to take pictures.

 Food
Eight Tiny Reindeer: This is a fun theme restaurant at which all diners are given pajamas to wear while being

served by "elves" in a Christmas setting. At the beginning of the evening, a ho-hoing "Santa" appears, leading eight live reindeer on a sleigh through the dining room straight into the kitchen. These same reindeer later emerge, wrapped in "gift boxes," in generous hot and tender portions. It's clever and distinctively Swedish twist on the Christmas theme that's fun and educational for the whole family!

Cafeé Tjänkenschungenätt: Located on Schöngerenackavaemmetan at Sibbergångstorbergenväg, a delicious heebenhårenstak away from heebenhårenstak, where the homemade svarkenagenoogen will make you lick your möllenvåängats clean, and we're not just pulling your kirbenoobenägens!

COPENHAGEN

Copenhagen, when it's not unbearably cold,[2] is a delightful, vibrant city best known as the **hometown of Hans Christian Andersen**. Of all the folklore surrounding Hans's life, one hears very little about younger brother **Franz Christian Andersen**, who was always trying to one-up his brother's ideas but could never quite capture his magic. Take **"The Even Uglier Duckling,"** about a young misfit whose looks are *really* made fun of, so he flies away for the winter. Imagine the other ducks' surprise when he shows up at the class reunion and it turns out he was never really a duck at all but has blossomed into a full-grown **gray walrus**, who promptly devours them. Then there was **"The Even Littler Mermaid,"** about a small, shy half-fish who has dreamed all her life of living on land, so one day she climbs onto a beach to her freedom. Here she is found and greeted by none other than the Even Uglier Duckling, who promptly devours her.

 **Sights**

Well, there's the Little Mermaid Statue, inspired by the **Hans Christian Andersen** story. You can also explore the winding cobblestone streets of the Old City, many of which **Hans**

---

[2]July 18, 1908

Christian Andersen himself walked down. And you'll feel just like **Hans Christian Andersen** as you pick out a crusty alley to sleep in, because today, not even a resurrected **Hans Christian Andersen** with royalty rights could afford the hotels here!

Food

Sample Copenhagen's delicious **street food**, much of which by the looks of it dates back to the time of **Hans Christian Andersen.**

As you've probably guessed by now, the *last* thing that we'd want to say about Copenhagen is that

> **it's one big nauseating commercialized
> shrine to a two-bit children's story writer**

There's so much more we want to tell you about this *incredibly diverse* yet traditional city. But unfortunately, one of Copenhagen's biggest traditions is that it is actually located in **Denmark**.

Poland
The Easy Target

Poland ain't no land of laughter,
'Spite of all them jokes we know.
We think it must be named after
Mr. Edgar Allan Po.

BUT FIRST,
A WORD ABOUT EASTERN EUROPE

"Go to Eastern Europe!" everyone raves after visiting. "Go to Eastern Europe! We don't want to be the only ones who were fooled!"

Back in the heady, carefree days of the Cold War, news programs devoted as much coverage to the problems of Eastern Europe as they did to the problems of ear wax disposal. The average American would have identified Bulgaria as, if anything at all, a teenage eating disorder. But after watching the 1989 revolutions, people suddenly found themselves much more enlightened about Eastern Europe, knowing for the first time, for example, what city the Berlin Wall was in,[1] and quick to correct others that Bull Garia is not an eating disorder at all, but is in fact the World Wrestling Federation's new Eastern European character.[2]

Soon Eastern Europe became a popular alternative destination for travelers. We're here to let the air out of this idea, and come to think of it, it could use a good airing out.

Why go to Eastern Europe? For the **culture**? Listen, after 40 years of Communist Bloc–head rule, the only culture Eastern Europe has left is **agri-**.

For the **entertainment**? Unless you're into sludge sculpture contests or Gulag bus tours, you'll have to settle for hanging out with natives in rundown bars and talking about local events, such as **smog**.

To meet the **people**? Well, they are a lovely group of folks. Every single one of them *we* met greeted us with the traditional introduction, "You're from America? Do you **surf**?"

Because it's **inexpensive**? Well, sure, one could live here for a month on a single UNICEF box. But frankly—and we say this with all due respect to Eastern Europeans—it's a **stinkhole**. Besides, if you're so concerned about saving money, then (not to burst your brain cells but) *why are you going to Europe in the first place*?

It's getting better, mind you. They have **McDonald's** restaurants there now. **MTV** is being consumed at record rates. And over 10,000,000,000 **young Americans** are pouring into Prague each day, all of whom figure, "Oh, I'll get by teaching English." Er . . . to

[1]Berlin
[2]paired with Hugo Slavia in tag-team matches

whom? There are now more American English teachers in Prague than there are native citizens.

It's an exciting region that is currently experiencing the dry heaves of democratic change. To give you a better perspective, we now proudly present to you Poland, our token Eastern European country. . . .

POLAND
VITAL INFORMATION

Currency in use: None

Dominant stereotype: Grumpy, pear-shaped, old, sausage-munching crones

Official motto: "If you can't beat 'em, get annexed by 'em"

Theme song: [sung to the tune of "Rawhide"]

> "Poland, Poland, Poland . . .
> Each lung has a hole in
> it from all the coal an'
> Oxides!"

For fun: Placing bets on which direction their next invaders will come from

Contributions to American culture: Jokes, jokes, jokes!

Ugly American visits, returns with: Great haste

Overall rating (−10 to 0): −8

How to sound like you've really, truly been there: "Sucked. Leave me alone. I don't wanna talk about it."

Poland? You're thinking about *Poland?* Not setting our sights *too* high now, are we?

We have enough **dirt** on Poland to make a landfill out of the

Grand Canyon. Not that Poland doesn't have enough dirt of its own; after forty years of Communist pollution, they should probably just stick a gigantic Mr. Yuck-Mouth sticker over the whole country and abandon ship. When locals see the phrase "Polish landscape," they're not sure if it's a description or a suggestion. Even the opposition group here was named **Solid-air-ity**.

History

Anyway, about a thrillion zillion years ago, Poland was a major force in Europe, which we are sure provided fodder for all sorts of jokes in China. A couple centuries back, though, it was conquered by its neighbors and chopped into little bite-sized pieces that were divvied up and used as compost facilities or sold off in undeveloped lots through shady real estate companies. But Life After Poland just wasn't that fun, so after World War I, the country was recreated and christened with its official nickname, **the Piñata State**.

Then came the famous Russo-German tag-team occupation years. Germans. Russians. Germans. Russians. Poor Poland got the *borscht* kicked out of it. The Germans left. The Russians stayed. And Poland once again had to put up with uninvited guests.

> In its past few centuries, Poland has become known as "the **airplane lavatory** of Europe"— dirty, subject to turbulence, and almost constantly occupied.

The Commies set up the Poland chapter of their ever-popular **Bloc Party**, did the Evil Empire thing, drank all their vodka, and *whew*, let's just say they won't be getting their cleaning deposit back. The rebel force **Solidarity** formed in 1980, and was successful enough to force the government to declare **martial law** for eight years, to which most Poles responded, "Well what the hell were we living under before? Direct democracy?"

So why did Solidarity survive all that time? Two reasons:

1) You are what you eat. Poles eat beet soup, fatty kielbasa sausage. . . . No wonder they're so good at **revolting**—that's the only kind of food they eat.

2) Poles have that unsinkable **Polish character**, best described as some genetic crossbreeding between Grumpy and Dopey. The Poles are **born grumps**. Maybe it's the weather.[3] Maybe it's the rough history. Maybe all that grease has clogged up their cheek muscles. But we'd rather relive *junior high* than be stuck in a room full of angry Poles.

 For a dramatic reenactment of its history, consider reading *Poland* by James "Rand McNally" Michener, a veritable atlas in the world of fiction writers. You know, he wrote *Texas, Haiti, Alaska.* . . . We just hope he never runs out of interesting ideas, or we'll be subjected to epic sagas like *Lichtenstein* or *Fresno* or *That Little Nubbin of Land on the Tip of Minnesota.*

 ## Understanding Those Peculiar Natives
This just in: The Polish aren't **grumpy**; it was all a terrible misunderstanding. Y'see, when Polish people respond to their name, instead of saying "Yes?" they use a word that sounds to us like "No." Even worse, their expression for "What?" or "Eh?" or "Huh?" sounds like "So?" Thus whenever we asked for directions to a sight we were trying to get to, such as **Western Europe**, the following conversation would occur:

Me:　Excuse me. . . .
Pole:　No.
Me:　No? Gee whiz, I haven't even asked you anything yet!
Pole:　So?

---

[3]"We have a carbon monoxide front coming in from the east, with increasing sulfur later in the day giving way to a light acid rain sometime before sundown."

Me: So, don't you think you're being rude?
Pole: So?
Me: So, why don't you and your whole cabbage-eating country go find another iron curtain to hide behind! I've had enough! [Irate author stomps off, leaving confused Pole behind him.]

Culture
But really now, does Poland deserve its tuna-brain reputation? Well, those worried about spreading unfair stereotypes will be relieved to discover that . . . yes, it does. During our overextended stay, we discovered what are collectively known as

POLISHISMS: WHY THE JOKES ARE JUSTIFIED

• For stomachaches, headaches, congestion, minor amputations, and stuffy-head-fever-so-you-can-rest problems, what is the Polish remedy of choice? Coal. That's right, little tablets of compressed petroleum. Poles really dig this medicine,[4] and it's a great example of the utilization of local resources. But we want to know what the local remedy for **stomach cancer** is.

• Polish currency was the recent undisputed champ of the International Most Resembles **Monopoly Money** Competition, sweeping both the appearance and value categories. Their 50-zl bill is worth half a cent in good ol' Am'r'c'n money. *Zl* must be short for **zilch**.

• Poles observe the day before Easter in the holy ritual of sneaking up and throwing **buckets of water** on each other. Camp children have their own variation called **green night**, when they go around smearing **toothpaste** on the counselors. It's a shame to see their sense of humor stuck back in '40s slapstick while our tastes have been allowed to mature to the level of, say, Beavis and Butthead.

• We were talking once with a Polish woman who was anxious to try out her English. Speaking of her compatriots' financial trou-

---

[4]Er . . . they really dig *up* this medicine.

bles, she nodded and said knowingly, "Well, if you can't stand the heat, get out of the chicken." We here at *Don't Go* believe that this one statement justifies **every single Polish joke** that has **ever** been told in **the history of humankind**.

Practical Information

As you enter Poland, the **hard-nosed ex-Commie border guard** will make you show your passport and fill out a form that looks something like the one on page 152.

WARSAW

Just when you thought things couldn't get any worse . . . they get even Warsaw.

Sights

What distinguishes Warsaw's **Old Town** from the 93,000,000 other Old Towns in Europe is the fact that it was **built after 1945**. No kidding. World War II destroyed their *old* Old Town, and so they decided to build a *new* Old Town. They did an excellent job right down to the **ruins** and **dangerous structural defects** that existed before, so exercise caution in this area.

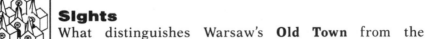

Food

As a rule we never visit a Polish restaurant without reservations. Not that Polish restaurants are difficult to get into; we just always have reservations about eating Polish.

Polish **kielbasa** comes in many varieties, much like the different Cycle foods we have here in America. By far the most recommended way to try these sausages is **vicariously**, so bring a friend.

Our only other experience with Polish food that can be described without the use of low-pitched digestive noises was at the **Restaurant Maryla** in Warsaw, where we had a vase with **plastic flowers** on the table. Just for kicks, we peeked into the vase. It was filled with **water**. That *killed* us.

PSOWJIE![5]
WELCOME TO POLAND

1. I am

- ☐ a returning resident of Poland. Have mercy.
- ☐ just visiting. Boy am I dumb or what? *(Please fill out section 2.)*
- ☐ invading. *(Please fill out sections 2 and 3 and take a number.)*

2. Nonresidents are allowed to bring into the country up to 100 cigarettes and no more than three bottles of liquor per person, preferably vodka.

A. Are you bringing cigarettes and/or liquor into the country?

- ☐ yes *(Please go on to question B.)*
- ☐ no *(Please answer question B anyway.)*

B. Can we have some?
- ☐ yes
- ☐ no

3. (*The following information is confidential and used for settling bets only.*) From which direction are you invading?

_____

Invader Warning: There is currently a 2–3 month waiting list + processing time for conquering Poland. If you are in a rush, may we suggest France?

Notice: Due to the backlog, we can no longer provide weapons for our invaders. Please be sure you have all necessary arms before *entering the country.*

---

[5]a Polish word, meaning "sucker"

Gourmet items like **fruit** are still something of a novelty here, and those crazy Polish *loooooove* **bananas**. One young woman actually had the audacity to suggest that their fruit is better than ours in the States. She said, "Huh, we got some fruit here that was grown in California once, and it was all rotted and brown and awful! I don't know how you could eat fruit like that."

"We don't," I said. "We ship it all to Poland."

 ## Accommodations

A popular option in Eastern Europe is **staying in private homes**, which will make you feel like you're **one of the family**, except that in Poland mothers tell you, "Now if you're *real good*, I'll let you go to bed without any supper." And if you're not real good, you'll be in the **bathroom** for the rest of your stay.

 ## Europe Close-Up:
European A-Commode-Ations

Don't Go! Don't Go to the Bathroom!

"Now, hold it . . ." you may say. And that's all that we're saying too. Hold it—until you get back to the States, if possible, or at least until you can get to the airplane lavatory. If you absolutely have to visit a European john before you return to the saniflushed shores of the good old U.S.A., at least read these warnings first so you won't get caught with your pants down:

Warning #1: The further east or south you go in Europe, the more you'll need to import your own toiletries—razors, tampons, non-rump-tearing toilet paper, the Sunday comics, soap-on-a-rope—to maintain your high standards. This continues all the way to Russia or southern Spain, by which point it will be necessary to bring with you the entire **toilet**.

Warning #2: European toilets can be different from the American

Standard. This is due to THE NUMBER ONE SECRET FEAR OF ALL EUROPEANS. It is a horrible possibility more frightening to a European than that of a **Russian invasion**, **revisionist history**, even the thought of **Garth Brooks** buying Austria and inviting the entire state of Tennessee to move in. Are you ready? Presenting now, for the first time in print, THE NUMBER ONE SECRET FEAR OF ALL EUROPEANS is

splashing

They can't *stand* the thought of it. For some reason, the idea of a little *eau de toilet* splashing up onto their pristine privvies puts them into a state of shock.

And to think: These are the same people who get such a kick out of using **berets**.[6]

One Italian described to us how he would lay strips of toilet paper across the entire bowl leaving a hole in the middle *juuust* big enough for the essentials to get through, all to make sure he'd stay dry.

And **those nutty Germans** have changed the **entire design** of their toilets specifically to eliminate splashing. How'd they do it?

Well, instead of being shaped like a bowl on the inside, German toilets have a raised porcelain platform that extends about two-thirds of the way inside the bowl, and then curves downward into a small passage leading below in front. When you do your dirty deed, the stuff lands on this waterless platform, thus preventing any drips, drops, or plops. Ideally, when you flush, the water rushes over this platform, pushing everything over the brink and down the tubes.

Ideally. But every so often, one gets a Rambo-strength piece of poop that *clings on to the platform*, even through multiple flushes and strong words of encouragement. At this point, it is necessary to coax our friendly piece of feces over the edge using the long brush that is conveniently placed next to every German toilet.

Then one has to scrub off whatever little Rambo bits might be left hanging on.

Afterwards, one must *clean* the brush. All this just to prevent a few drops of tainted water from touching the sacred rumps of the Teutonic tribes.

----

[6]Bidets. Sorry.

During our travels, we met a Mr. Timothy Bailey of Dearborn, Michigan, who, when we mentioned the brush, suddenly said, "Oh man . . . I thought that brush was for cleaning your back in the shower." That's Tim Bailey from Michigan.

Warning #3: The only **showers** you'll find in European homes are those little handheld WaterPik jobbies, which wouldn't be so bad if Europeans had discovered the remarkable principles behind the **shower curtain**.

This was the case in the home we stayed at in Poland, and we had to play Twister with ourselves in the bathtub in order to keep the floor somewhat dry, at least until we dropped the showerhead outside the tub.[7] After our hosts finished draining the bathroom, we were kindly invited to find another residence for the following night.

 And remember: You're an American going into the bathroom, you're an American leaving the bathroom, but you're a-peein' while you're in the bathroom, so don't stay too long.

KRAKOW

Krakow, affectionately known as the Newark of Europe, is a cozy little town in southern Poland where, if you're as lucky as one of our researchers, you'll be **mugged** and **beaten** by **young, bald Easterner skinhead locals** with nothing on their hands but free time and heavy chains. Tipping is not necessary.

---

[7]OK, OK, we were pretending to sing into it, and it slipped out of our grasp during a high note.

Sights

Krakow is home of **Kosciol Mariacki Church**, whose altar-piece, according to *Let's Go,* "is ceremoniously unveiled at noon each day." We have this mental picture of Polish locals crowding up in front of the tarp just before noon every day, wondering to themselves what could possibly be underneath it *this* time, and squealing with delight when it's unveiled and they all shout in unison, "It's the altarpiece again!"

Krakow is also one of only about 12 cities that have **the largest square in all of Europe**. Here and elsewhere you will find an **open market** where you can buy such native crafts as **ultra-thin, square-packaged T-shirts** with off-center writing that says things like I SURVIVED KRAKOW, POLAND. Keep your eyes peeled! You may even see some *real Russians*, but do not point or otherwise provoke them.

BE BOLD! BE STUPID! BE AMERICAN!

Oh, OK, it's your only chance, go ahead and provoke them. If you see some Russians, jump up and down in a circle around them going "Woo, woo! We won! We won!" If they pull out their muskets to shoot you, please do us a favor and keep still.

This market, we imagined, would finally give us a chance to engage in the un-American-except-when-buying-a-car practice of **haggling**.

Real Testimony: Barter Luck Next Time

I'd really looked forward to haggling with the natives and the feeling of empowerment that comes from walking away with a worthless object for which you paid only *four times* as much as it's worth instead of six times.

Alas, the Polish have caught on to Western-style capitalism much too quickly, and the experience was not as pleasant as I'd imagined:

WHAT I BELIEVED WOULD HAPPEN

Me: How much is this here balsawood carving of a herring?

Vendor: 30,000 zloty, sir.

Me: I'll give you 4,000.

Vendor: Four thousand? But this is the finest balsawood! My sick, dying grandmother would climb into her grave and roll over in it if she heard your offer! Make it 25,000 zloty, sir, because I can see you have excellent taste.

Me: Fie! This carving is not worth a rabid flea on the mangy coat of the great aunt of my worst enemy's dog! But I will give you 8,000 for it.

Vendor: Oh, you are a hard-driving bargain man, sir. Did I not tell you that this is the last one of its kind? A rare item, destined to increase in value, much like your American limited-edition Star Trek plates! I'll give it to you for 20,000 sir, because you are a very special man, but do not let others know I am giving you this.

Me: I swear by the Pope's hat I must have lost my wits, but look, I'll give you 10,000. That's it.

Vendor: OK, OK, 10,000 zloty, but please sir, never come back to my booth again. You are much too smooth a bargainer man! [carefully gives me herring]

WHAT ACTUALLY HAPPENED

Me: How much is this here balsawood carving of a herring?

Vendor: 30,000 zloty, sir.

Me: I'll give you 4,000.

Vendor: Like hell you will, sir.

Me: OK . . . Um, fie? Uh, I'll give you 8,000.

Vendor: Please, kindly go screw yourself, sir.

Me: Look, I'll give you 10,000. That's it.

Vendor: You'll give me shit, sir. The price is 30,000 zloty.

Me: [whining] Um, I don't *knooow*. . . .

Vendor: Hurry up and buy the damn herring. You're wasting my time.

Me: Oh, OK. Here's 30,000 zloty.

Vendor: What? No tip? You cheapskate! [throws herring in my face]

But maybe we're being too harsh. A trip to Poland really can change you. . . . Changed *us* to vegetarian hermits.

Conclusion

If there's just one thing you walk away from this book knowing besides CPR, which you really should learn because the life you save could be your own, then it's *Don't Go: Europe!* This should be pretty clear by now.

But there are bound to be some naysayers in the audience, Europhiliacs who will retort, "Bah! If it weren't for Europe, just think of all the troubles the world would have!" Well, we did. Troubles like where to go swimming in the new, improved, *really* big Mediterranean. Troubles like what should the three remaining members of NATO get on their pizza now that there are no whiny countries to defend and they have a little extra cash? Troubles like who's going to write all those embarrassing pop songs now that Sweden's gone? Who's going to put ketchup on their pizzas now that Poland's gone? Who's going to be French now that France is gone? Nobody? Good!

"Tut, tut," you say. "There must be some bad things about having no Europe." Well, we thought about that, too, and came up with this list:

1. No Toblerone

There you go. That's why we're starting an overfunded, highly influential, corrupt Washington lobby group known simply as LGRERNJIIHIGA (Let's Get Rid of Europe Right Now by Just Ignoring It and Hoping It Goes Away). LGRERNJIIHIGA will fight for laws banning any talk or conscious thought of Europe, encourage the substitution of vague euphemisms such as "ol' you-know-where" and "upper-upper Africa" when it must be referred to, and suggest alternative locales to congressmen when they decide they must go on an official Fact-Finding Tour of Some Warm Climate with your tax money. Soon people everywhere will be saying, "I'm proud to be a member of LGRERNJIIHIGA!"

What can you do to help? One very important thing: **Buy more copies of this book**. Spread the word! That way, we here at *Don't Go* can afford another Riviera trip for, um, research purposes. Yes, we know, we *are* quite the martyr. To sum it all up, Gesundheit America, never read the travel section, learn CPR, and remember: The only winning move is not to go.

Chris Harris grew up in Connecticut, but it just wasn't far away enough. "Ew! I'm touching the same ocean as the British!" he often exclaimed during his family's beach trips. So he moved to San Francisco, where he currently lives, drawing pictures and working on the Mediocre American Novel. He does not usually wear flags.

Chris's Belgo-Hungarian cousin, Jean-Louis Philippe Von Harris, served as an invaluable information source and field researcher for this book, while Chris himself hung out at the Euro Disney arcade. Jean-Louis enjoys Marxist literature, angst, and scouring the Bible for signs of ABBA's second coming.